Praise for *Ins*

"Need-to-read inside information and line—the best source in the business." – LLP

"The *Inside the Minds* series is a valuable probe into the thoughts, perspectives, and techniques of accomplished professionals..." – Chuck Birenbaum, Partner, Thelen Reid & Priest

"Aspatore has tapped into a goldmine of knowledge and expertise ignored by other publishing houses." – Jack Barsky, Managing Director, Information Technology and CIO, ConEdison Solutions

"Unlike any other publisher—actual authors that are on the front lines of what is happening in industry." – Paul A. Sellers, Executive Director, National Sales, Fleet and Remarketing, Hyundai Motor America

"A snapshot of everything you need..." – Charles Koob, Co-Head of Litigation Department, Simpson Thacher & Bartlet

"Everything good books should be—honest, informative, inspiring, and incredibly well written." – Patti D. Hill, President, BlabberMouth PR

"Great information for both novices and experts." – Patrick Ennis, Partner, ARCH Venture Partners

"A rare peek behind the curtains and into the minds of the industry's best." – Brandon Baum, Partner, Cooley Godward

"Intensely personal, practical advice from seasoned deal-makers." – Mary Ann Jorgenson, Coordinator of Business Practice Area, Squire, Sanders & Dempsey

"Great practical advice and thoughtful insights." – Mark Gruhin, Partner, Schmeltzer, Aptaker & Shepard PC

"Reading about real-world strategies from real working people beats the typical business book hands down." – Andrew Ceccon, CMO, OnlineBenefits Inc.

"Books of this publisher are syntheses of actual experiences of real-life, hands-on, front-line leaders—no academic or theoretical nonsense here. Comprehensive, tightly organized, yet nonetheless motivational!" – Lac V. Tran, Senior Vice President, CIO, and Associate Dean, Rush University Medical Center

"Aspatore is unlike other publishers...books feature cutting-edge information provided by top executives working on the front lines of an industry." – Debra Reisenthel, President and CEO, Novasys Medical Inc.

www.Aspatore.com

Aspatore Books is the largest and most exclusive publisher of C-Level executives (CEO, CFO, CTO, CMO, partner) from the world's most respected companies and law firms. Aspatore annually publishes a select group of C-Level executives from the Global 1,000, top 250 law firms (partners and chairs), and other leading companies of all sizes. C-Level Business Intelligence™, as conceptualized and developed by Aspatore Books, provides professionals of all levels with proven business intelligence from industry insiders—direct and unfiltered insight from those who know it best—as opposed to third-party accounts offered by unknown authors and analysts. Aspatore Books is committed to publishing an innovative line of business and legal books, those which lay forth principles and offer insights that, when employed, can have a direct financial impact on the reader's business objectives, whatever they may be. In essence, Aspatore publishes critical tools—need-to-read as opposed to nice-to-read books—for all business professionals.

Inside the Minds

The critically acclaimed *Inside the Minds* series provides readers of all levels with proven business intelligence from C-Level executives (CEO, CFO, CTO, CMO, partner) from the world's most respected companies. Each chapter is comparable to a white paper or essay and is a future-oriented look at where an industry/profession/topic is heading and the most important issues for future success. Each author has been carefully chosen through an exhaustive selection process by the *Inside the Minds* editorial board to write a chapter for this book. *Inside the Minds* was conceived in order to give readers actual insights into the leading minds of business executives worldwide. Because so few books or other publications are actually written by executives in industry, *Inside the Minds* presents an unprecedented look at various industries and professions never before available.

INSIDE THE MINDS

The Business of Toys and Games

*Top Executives on Launching New Products, Developing
a Recognizable Brand, and Competing for Shelf Space*

Published by Aspatore Inc.

For corrections, company/title updates, comments, or any other inquiries, please e-mail store@aspatore.com.

First Printing, 2006
10 9 8 7 6 5 4 3 2 1

ISBN-10: 1-59622-627-7
ISBN-13: 978-1-59622-627-2
Library of Congress Control Number: 2006940215

Inside the Minds Project Manager, Kristen Skarupa; edited by Michaela Falls; proofread by Eddie Fournier

The Business of Toys and Games

*Top Executives on Launching New Products, Developing
a Recognizable Brand, and Competing for Shelf Space*

CONTENTS

Putting Education First in the Toy and Game Industry

Thomas J. Kalinske

Vice Chairman and Former Chief Executive Officer

LeapFrog Enterprises, Inc.

After eleven years in business, our company has shown itself to be different than many others in the toy industry in that we consider ourselves to be mainly an education company, and only happen to sell some of our products to toy channels. Simply put, our company goal is to become the leading brand for educational products. At this time, we are in the children's market, but our ultimate goals are in fact much more broad. We would like to provide technology-based educational products for people of all ages, both in the United States and around the world.

In order to be sure we are meeting these goals, we measure ourselves internally as to how we are doing in our market share in the different markets we serve. We have educational products for children as young as zero to two years old, as well as the toddler age set, the pre-school and kindergarten age set, and the grade school age set. Market share becomes an important measure by which we can track ourselves in each of these groups.

Yet more important than simply measuring market share, we must be sure what we are doing is truly effective. For this, we have an outside advisory board of renowned educators from around the country that reviews everything we do to ensure it is educationally correct. Of course we also do our own research, and our research shows our products to be effective, but in this business it is important to bring in others for research and evaluation purposes. This provides a solid system of checks and balances.

LeapFrog's Vision

Our vision, which has remained the same for eleven years, is to become the leading brand for technology-based educational products for school, work, and home use for all ages around the world. This is a grandiose vision statement, and naturally it is a challenge to live up to it. Looking at ourselves now, eleven years after founding, we find we have a leading share of educational products in the United States, but we do not have a leading share in many other markets around the world. This means we have huge opportunities to grow.

On the one hand, we have a big vision for our company, but at the same time we are at this point only successful in the consumer products area. The school market is a very fragmented business, and we consider ourselves largely to provide supplemental materials to the school business. For example, we are not a Basal textbook publisher, but we offer products that supplement those Basal texts. At present, we are a minor player in that area with a 3 percent share, which leaves a great room for growth. In the workplace market, we offer products for Spanish speakers to learn English, particularly in the hospitality and restaurant business. Of course, that is just one segment of the workplace market, so again we have great opportunities ahead.

The Toy and Game Industry: Unique Considerations

The key characteristic of the toy and game industry is that it serves a very special audience, namely children. There are many issues we must be careful about that perhaps other industries do not. Children are generally considered a protected group, and this leads to some unusual safety issues, highly unusual child development issues, and even some very unusual advertising issues.

As an industry, we have adopted the children's advertising review guidelines for Internet and media advertising. Because it is very easy to mislead children through advertising and marketing, we have had to adopt very special rules to be sure such a thing does not occur. It is difficult for executives from other industries to grasp these issues instantly. Truly understanding the differences between marketing to children and marketing to thirty- to forty-year-old adults takes time in the business. Because we here at LeapFrog do in fact market to adults, we are in this regard at least somewhat different from the rest of the industry.

The most important way to stay on top of one's knowledge in the educational toy industry is to be constantly engaged with children. Watching how children learn or do not learn and remaining in communication with teachers and educators about their frustrations is critical. One of the most eye-opening experiences for me has been visiting schools in lower income areas of Berkley or Oakland and finding kindergarten teachers with twenty-three children in their classrooms. Among those twenty-three children as many as seven different languages might be spoken, and that teacher is still expected to perform to the same level as a teacher in Hillsborough, an affluent area, where household income in several $100,000 a year and every child speaks English. There are major obstacles faced by teachers today, particularly those in urban areas, and it is exciting for us to be involved in helping them to deal with those obstacles.

Research and Development

The decision of when to launch a new product comes down to the research that shows the product to be educationally effective. For example, we have developed great methods for helping children learn to read in English, all of which have been researched very effectively, and our Leap Pad series of hardware and software is a direct product of that. We also work to identify potential market opportunities. Reading is an ongoing opportunity, and recently we have begun to look to language education, both in terms of foreign languages for English speakers and English for non-English speakers around the world. Thus, the product launch cycle begins with evaluating the market, determining when the product can be ready for delivery, researching its effectiveness, and finally determining a launch plan.

Because we are a technology-based company, we are constantly looking for new technologies to help the educational process, which sets us apart from other toy companies. We always joke that we think of the folks at Mattel and Hasbro as the kinds of company that hears about the importance of phonics and decides to create a toy bus that simply recites the alphabet. Our research and development (R&D) process is considerably more in depth than that, and as a result our products are more complex. For example, we would bring in the concept of rhyming different letter sounds and combining separate letter sounds to make different sounds. We incorporate true teaching methods, like those used at UC Berkley or Stanford University, into our products; from there, we work with a university or independent groups to conduct research before deciding to bring the product to market.

One of the key issues we face is how to incorporate technology into a product while keeping it affordable. Unlike other companies, we develop our own integrated circuit chips—I guarantee that companies like Mattel and Hasbro do not, and in fact I have heard them call us crazy for doing so. Yet the reason we develop our own chips is simply the fact that there often is no existing chip that will do exactly what we want a product to do. Thus, we will have our R&D group develop a chip specifically for the educational content we want delivered—with the right visuals, with the right voice quality, and with the right sound modulation. All of that costs a good deal of money, but once we have done it, it gives us a distinct advantage over our competition.

In short, our R&D process is based on both consumer need and educational pedagogy requirements. Once those two things are combined, we must determine whether the consumer still wants the product, how it researches, and what its advantage over the competition is before we can determine our launch plan. It makes for a much longer R&D process than a typical toy company.

Understanding Consumer Need

We do considerable research to determine what our consumers want and what schools need. Of course, our research is generally conducted with mothers, which allows us to identify and understand their children's educational pain points. Early in our development as a company, it became very clear that helping children learn to read was a huge pain point for mothers. She did not feel that she knew how to teach reading, and she was very concerned about some of the shortcomings of school programs. She also knew intuitively that if her child did not read well by the third grade, there would be a very good chance that her child would be left behind in the educational process. If a child cannot read a math book, he cannot do math; if he cannot read a history book, he cannot understand history. This is where we focused our early efforts to help mothers resolve that pain point, and it made us relatively successful with our reading products.

A current pain point that has come up over and over again in our research is math. Many parents are very uncomfortable with their own memories of math instruction, and as a result are unsure of how to help their children learn, particularly as the children reach grades five through seven. If parents do not understand algebra themselves, it will be difficult for them to aid their children with pre-algebra and algebra schoolwork. We have made great efforts in our R&D department to address this issue, and we are now launching some products to help address the algebra pain point.

Of course, we must balance fulfilling the needs of the adults with creating a product that will be interesting to a child. We quickly learned that if we merely follow what the large education textbook companies do, chances are that our products would not hold the child's interest. If a mother spends money for a product her child ultimately is not interested in, she is not going to buy another one and we will have failed in our mission. We want a mother to be able to hand our product to her child without much being required on her part, and as the product walks the child through the process of learning algebra, perhaps it will rekindle her own memories at the same time. Ultimately, we must make our products interactive, interesting, and frankly fun for the children to engage with, or we will lose their interest and we will fail.

Creating Market Share

I have been in the toy industry for thirty-five years now. I was once chief executive officer of Mattel, Matchbox, and SEGA, so I know the space well. Throughout my history in the business, the standard belief was that although mothers claimed to want educational products, they were unwilling to pay for them. This was true in the '70s, '80s, and early '90s. When we formed the precursor company to LeapFrog, called Knowledge Universe, we agreed that thinking was wrong. We reasoned that the real problem was that companies such as Mattel or Sony are unable to make educational products mainly because if they spend the same resources on an entertainment title, they can most likely generate more revenue. Our theory was that if we dedicated ourselves 100 percent to education, we would have a shot at being successful and would not be diverted by the ease of making money in other areas.

Frankly, no one believed that we would be successful, and initially the retail buyers at Wal-Mart, Target, and Kmart did not even want to talk to us. They still believed mothers only claimed to want educational products, but would not actually buy them. For this reason, our early days were very trying, and we had to build distribution in small toy stores and bookstores in order to claw our way up the retail channels. The only exception was Toys R Us, which supported us from day one. When our products began to sell well, we were approached by other retailers. In this way, we created our own market and eventually expanded our retail presence.

The one area we may have taken market share from competitors was in educational software, since our increase in business coincided with the decline of that area of the market. We formed the company in 1996, and PC educational software began to decline just two years later. Educational software for the PC was a $900 million market in 1998; today it's declined to about $125 million. As we were growing so rapidly in that time period, some of our products likely took a little bit away from the PC software world. Ultimately, however, our success was due to the fact that our products offered an easier way for mothers to engage in education with their children, and the children actually learned while using our products and found the experience enjoyable.

Pricing Strategy

Economics in the toy industry is backwards: the more desirable a product is and the hotter it becomes in the peak selling season, the lower the price. This is of course the opposite of what economists predicted would occur over time, but it is a historic fact that retailers think of toys as a way of bringing customers into their stores. For example, back when Cabbage Patch dolls were red hot, retailers were selling them for $2 to $3 below what they themselves had paid. They were deliberately losing money simply because the product was in such short supply, and they knew that if they could promise consumers a Cabbage Patch doll, hoards of parents would come rushing to their stores. This would of course increase the chances that those same mothers would buy other products at the same time, meaning an indirect profit for the retailer from the loss incurred on Cabbage Patch dolls.

This phenomenon has never changed in the many years I have been in the toy industry. It always surprises me, but it always remains true: the hotter the product, the lower the profit a retailer will make on it. This also flies in the face of all the discussions between toy manufacturers and their retail partners, in which retailers typically ask for a 35 to 40 percent margin over the price. We try to accommodate our retailers—for example, selling our product at $6 so they can sell it for $10—because we understand that they want a return on their investment of space. However, if we sell a product to them at $16 with the idea that retailers will sell it for $20 and that item becomes hot in the market, those same retailers may eventually sell the product for as little as $15. The next year, they will complain to us about low profitability, but ultimately we have nothing to do with how such "hot" items are priced to the consumer.

At LeapFrog, we have a very broad price range for our key products. Our software is generally priced from $14.95 to $24.95, and our hardware platforms are priced anywhere from $29.95 to $99.95. Generally, we have a slightly higher-priced profile than the traditional toy company. Pricing is directly related to our margins, both internal and retail, and for this reason is carefully managed primarily by the financial and sales groups.

Return on Investment Metrics: Estimating the Life of a Product

When we are anticipating a rate of return on our R&D investments, we want to see a several 100 percent rate over the life of the product. In estimating the life of a product, we factor in saturation of the age group and of the new entrants to the market each year. One of the issues we face today is that our LeapPad product line has been in the market since 1998, and as such it is becoming somewhat long in the tooth. The core market LeapPad serves is the four- to seven-year-old age group, and we have penetrated almost 70 percent of that market. Our only real market opportunity for an older product like the LeapPad is the new entrants to the market each year, of which we must penetrate a reasonable percentage. If there are 4 million children entering the market every year, that number defines the size of the pool we are working with.

With this in mind, we try to estimate our life cycle to anticipate how it is going to progress, where the peak will be, and what the logical decline will be. From there, we must work to manage the life cycle we have predicted so that we can develop a suitable replacement. This is certainly the stage we have reached with the LeapPad at this point.

External Influences on Pricing Strategy

A major influence on pricing strategy is, of course, the competition. However, although we have competitors who pretend to offer similar products of similar educational quality, they in fact do not. As a result, they are able to charge less for their products than we do because they do not have the same R&D or research investment burdens that we do. We have accepted this fact, our retailers have accepted this fact, and to a large degree, I believe the parent purchaser has accepted this fact. We will always be a few dollars more than any comparable products in the marketplace, and our objective is to prove our educational value is worth those few dollars.

More importantly, our pricing strategies are impacted by the price of plastics and electronic components. Back when the cell phone business began to explode, there was a shortage in the supply of memory chips that had a negative impact on our company, as chip costs suddenly went through the roof. This had nothing to do with our business or our management, but rather was due to a seemingly unrelated industry. A similar situation has arisen these days with increasing oil prices, which has affected plastics pricing and shipping costs. Normally we update our prices yearly, but unusual external factors such as these can necessitate updating twice a year or more.

Marketing Strategies: Shifting the Emphasis from Cost to Quality

For retailers, we offer incentives of the same sort that are common with all consumer products. If a retailer grows shelf space with us, we may offer a greater discount; if a retailer advertises, we certainly offer coop advertising incentives; and if a retailer is opening new stores and must build new displays, we provide incentives for that as well.

We also provide incentives directly to our consumers. We do tie-ins with other consumer manufacturers, most often with cereal and beverage companies or, in the case of our infant and baby products, with other baby product manufacturers such as Gerber, Kimberly Clark or Johnson & Johnson. This can be either a coupon cross-promotion or perhaps a limited time premium. For example, LeapFrog products were featured on Quaker Oats/Tropicana Orange Juice packages (with multiple purchases you could receive free Leapster products). We also in-packet LeapFrog music CDs in Kimberly Clark's Huggies diapers to introduce LeapFrog to moms. Currently our FLY product is featured on Cheetos snack packages.

The Social Role of the Educational Company

I suspect that many people who have not been in the business for long do not realize that we are truly a product-driven industry. We need to have many new products every year to continue the excitement in our space. This not only ensures that we have something new to sell, but also drives consumers into stores to buy the products we invented years ago. Thus, the innovation factor is critical for the toy industry in general.

Specifically on the education side of our business, another vital factor is effectiveness. So many countries now face an educational crisis across a number of different measurements. One of the most common measurements in this country is the National Assessment of Educational Progress test given in public schools across the nation. The test has found that we have not improved our children's reading, math, or science scores for thirty years. A vast majority of children from the third to eighth grade are not reading or doing math at grade level—in fact, a full 70 percent of eighth grade children are below grade level in math skills. We will be unable to compete effectively as a country unless this issue is addressed. At LeapFrog we are developing and marketing products to help solve this problem.

The greatest advice I can offer from an educational standpoint is to make certain that the product you offer actually moves the needle, and actually improves the performance of children in their schools. I believe that, as purveyors of education, we have an unusual opportunity to make learning fun and interesting for children and to change the way our children are performing at a national level. Keep this in mind always, and make sure what you do truly works.

Key People

The people with whom I work most closely change depending upon the problems that we are facing and the time of the year. I always work very closely with the R&D group and the marketing group to define future product needs, to explore areas of future investment, and to track the progress of the products currently underway. For example, at this time we are finishing our 2007 product development and so our efforts are divided between making certain that we have all the details polished for the 2007 line while at the same time working three to four months into the beginning of the 2008 line. Both the R&D and marketing groups are critical to the process.

I also spend a good deal of time with the financial group reviewing our financial progress. I meet bi-monthly with the financial group reviewing our sales, gross margin progress, and net profit. The chief financial officer and I review and sign off on every product we formally put into the line. Monthly, the chief financial officer and I examine actuals to goals, sales, gross margin, costs/expenses by budget center, and net profit. We also meet with the executives in charge of each revenue and expense area to discuss their progress.

The key characteristic I look for in my team members is a high intellect. We pride ourselves on having a group of people who do not come exclusively from the toy, education, or software development industries. Rather, we look for a good blend of highly intelligent people from several different disciplines.

A second key characteristic is a passion for improving education both domestically and abroad. We have found that if someone lacks passion for improving the lives of children and adults alike, their chances of success at our company over time is low. Given the enthusiasm of the rest of our team, those who lack passion for improving education will simply not fit in.

I often advise my team members not to focus too much on the short term. Focusing on the long term ensures that we are doing the right thing for our different audiences, we are solving different pain points for our customers, and we will bring lasting benefit to the marketplace.

Difficult Situations

We have faced a number of difficult situations in our business. Our company grew rapidly as a developer and marketer of educational products, but we did not spend enough time on important issues such as our ability to manufacture and ship our products. For years, we relied upon outside vendors for contract manufacturing, warehousing, information technology systems and distribution, which sometimes led to problems. We have spent the last two years completely redoing our supply chain, from our manufacturers themselves, to our shipping methods, to our information technology systems for integrating the ordering, manufacturing, and shipping processes. These supply chain issues have demanded a great deal of my time for the past two years, but it is necessary in order to save time, costs, and trouble in the future.

The supply chain issue was certainly a shock to us. We had been relying on supposed experts, an entire group of companies whose purpose is to serve as distribution centers and manage the flow of the product, and we were quite surprised to find that some of the people we had chosen early on were simply not satisfying the requirements of our retail partners. We were unable to ship to Wal-Mart and Target in an accurate and timely fashion, and we quickly realized that we had to take a greater hand in the process. Our solution was to install Oracle, one of the major enterprise systems, and train people internally. It was a difficult and eye-opening experience, because it required us to learn a whole new language, a whole new system, a whole new way of entering data and of managing the process.

One of the other difficult issues we have faced has had to do with other companies copying our products. We spend millions of dollars on the R&D stage only to have competitors copy our technology and bring out lower-priced versions, both in the United States and in international markets. We have had to pursue legal actions, which is both difficult and costly. In China especially, the government will help to put a stop to knockoffs in one location, but they will very quickly arise elsewhere. It is painful for us to have spent so much money perfecting the technology and the educational curriculum, only to have others copy it without spending a nickel on it themselves.

Finally, being a public company today at our size can be a difficult issue in itself. We are not a particularly large company, and with the quarterly requirements and Sarbanes-Oxley requirements, it takes a great deal of effort and continuous training to comply with the various New York Stock Exchange and Sarbanes-Oxley requirements. This is compounded by the fact that we maintain a long-term perspective, and as such we try to ignore the quarterly pressure in order to focus on the ultimate benefit to the consumer.

Looking Forward

I believe that as the industry continues to evolve in the coming years, consolidation will continue. One of the great things about the toy industry in general is that it is a marvelous place for bright entrepreneurs to build a company on an idea, and we have a constant flow of new companies and new products emerging. Of course, as they get larger, bigger companies begin to take interest and often seek to acquire them. I see this as a healthy process, and I believe we will continue to see big companies acquiring smaller companies, but we will also see many new companies being formed and enjoying success.

Technology will also come to play a bigger and bigger part in the industry at large. The first chip ever to be used in a toy was sometime in the mid-1970s, and so it has been only twenty-five or thirty years since electronics were introduced into the industry. The advances that have been made since then have been remarkable. Today, we have dolls that emulate real babies, as well as learning technology offered by companies like ourselves. I believe downloadable products from the Internet will be an increasingly important trend moving forward, which will continue to blur the lines between toys and electronic products. Clearly marketing products and services online will become much more important. So will a company's ability to be in constant touch with its consumers and to personalize products online with new content. The Internet will change the business in ways we are only beginning to understand.

Finally, I believe the United States will continue to dominate the global toy industry. Competitors in other markets seem unable to grow in our markets, whereas U.S. companies seem able to grow all over the world. I do not expect this to change in the coming years.

Thomas J. Kalinske serves as LeapFrog's vice chairman on the board of directors. He served as chief executive officer from February 2004 to July 2006 and previously served in that capacity from September 1997 to March 2002. He has served on the board of directors since September 1997 and was the chairman of the board of directors from September 1997 to February 2004. From 1996 to February 2004, Mr. Kalinske served as the president of Knowledge Universe (now renamed Krest LLC), a private company focused on building leading companies in areas relating to education, technology and career management, and the improvement of individual and corporate performance. From 1990 to 1996, he served as president and chief executive officer of Sega of America. Prior to that, he was president and chief executive officer of the Universal Matchbox Group from 1987 to 1990. Prior to that, he served as president and co-chief executive officer of Mattel Inc. from 1985 to 1987 and in other senior management positions at Mattel from 1972 to 1985.

Mr. Kalinske has served as chairman of the Toy Manufacturers Association of America, and in 1997, he was inducted into the Toy Industry Hall of Fame. He is the non-executive deputy chairman of the board of Spring Group plc, an information technology services company in the United Kingdom. Mr. Kalinske is a past board member of the National Education Association Foundation for the Improvement of Education, the Milken Family Foundation, and the RAND Education Board.

He earned a B.S. from the University of Wisconsin, and an M.B.A. from the University of Arizona.

Kids II:
Innovation at Play

Ryan Gunnigle
President and Chief Executive Officer
Kids II

The primary benefit of working within the toys and games industry, particularly the infant product category we focus on, is the happiness we bring to moms and babies. It is extremely rewarding to know your product delivers intangible benefits—joy, laughter, fun.

From a business perspective, running a toys and games company is probably pretty similar to running any other type of company—other than the hyper-speed of product development and innovation. Even the staples of our industry are constantly reinvented to meet consumer needs. Babies are the core user of our products. That makes for a shorter product life cycle because they grow and change so much, so quickly. And look at consumer trends. Today's moms are always looking for better, easier solutions, especially when it comes to their babies. It's the nature of today's society. Not only that, we have a new consumer every nine months. Therefore, flexibility is the key to operating a toy company successfully, alongside maintaining speed and dealing with cost management principles. Many of our brands are sold in the mass channel. Cost management is critical when servicing key retailers such as Tesco, Wal-Mart, Target, and so on. We constantly monitor and manage cost areas such as raw materials, freight, logistics, and so on.

The Goals of the Chief Executive Officer

My goal as chief executive officer (CEO) of Kids II is to continue to spark innovation, support our ongoing growth, and create a culture of collaboration where it is fun to come to work each and every day. Of course we have many processes in place to help us realize our financial and strategic goals, from monthly management meetings to our intranet that allows us to communicate information centrally to all departments in real time. The toy category really requires daily, even hourly, management, as the industry is incredibly fast paced. In order to move faster, we place the information in everyone's hands so they can develop and run their businesses most effectively.

My overarching vision for the company is to:

- Get everyone in our company to think globally.
- Create an environment that attracts the top talent in all areas of the business. We offer world-class benefits and compensation on par with the biggest companies, diverse career opportunities within a

smaller but globally expanding business, not to mention flexible work hours, reward and recognition programs, entrepreneurial culture, casual dress code, flexible health spending, and 401K benefits.

- Use our company-wide communication of metrics and performance in real time as a checks and balances method. With global real-time reporting for the entire company we can constantly track key metrics and performance and quickly adjust our strategy when needed.

- Monitor our three-year plan, which includes agreed upon objectives and strategies, by department. Our strategy evolves, based on marketplace changes.

- Make sure the company is working within our core values and principles—honesty, integrity, and respect.

The three things I do that have the biggest direct financial impact in terms of adding value to my company are:

1. Maintain a fun, positive outlook; I do not believe in finger-pointing. I also give people room to excel and invest in our people.
2. Create a positive environment and vision for the company, based on the business climate in all our divisions. Great staff members support this vision and are responsible for the growth of the organization.
3. Focus on creating great products. I love product and strategic marketing and work hard at it. It's absolutely critical that we know our consumer, create an array of products that meet her unmet needs, and communicate our product benefits to her. All of that has to be right before there can even be a sale. We also need to understand our customers' requirements and the goods that they need.

A Global Marketplace

Maintaining this overarching vision is important, because from a global standpoint our business model has changed rapidly in the last three to four years. Five years ago we identified that we needed to go international because of the dwindling number of U.S. retailers. In order to become less dependent on those remaining U.S. retailers, we felt it was critical to expand our distribution.

Fortunately, we were able to leverage our U.S. volume and economies to go international and get better pricing for the smaller markets we were moving into—the United Kingdom, other European countries, Mexico, Canada, and Australia. We are much more competitive than some of the smaller competitors in those markets, so this proved to be a big opportunity for us. We also applied our strengths in other areas such as information technology and customer service to help us succeed.

We deal with an increasing number of multinational retailers, such as Wal-Mart, Mothercare, and Toys-R-Us. Fortunately we are able to work with them in a global consistent manner in terms of servicing their business needs, including product development, information technology, consumer services, and so on. These large retailers also want to leverage their U.S. volume to make their smaller markets more competitive; and they want to get the best prices possible. In essence, we help these larger retailers achieve their goals to be much more competitive in their overseas ventures.

A Successful Leadership Plan

Our corporate mission is to develop our brands and team globally and become the leader in baby products through innovation. We are constantly trying to challenge the status quo and do things better.

My vision for Kids II is to deliver innovation by constantly reinventing our staples and basic processes. Our award-winning Around We Go! ™ Activity Station is a perfect case study for how static categories can benefit from reinvention. The Bright Starts™ Around We Go! ™ revolutionized the "activity saucer" category, featuring an innovative product design that grows with baby. We placed the seat on the outside rather than the inside so babies could cruise around the play table. The seat then comes off to become an activity table for toddlers giving the product a much longer life.

My leadership plan is to collaborate with the best brains in the business. We have an unbelievably strong senior management team including vendor management and process, product development and business development, sales and marketing, and finance and accounting—and they play an integral role in running the company. I try to focus on my strengths and allow our executive managers to do the same. Developing our people is a top priority. We focus on celebrating wins and avoid finger-pointing on our losses.

In order to create an environment that attracts and retains top talent, I spend a lot of time researching what can be done from a human resources perspective to make our employees' lives better. We offer a very enjoyable office environment that includes Ping-Pong tables and pinball machines that employees use in their spare time. Every month we take a day to play arcade games and air hockey; we recently had an employee talent show as well. Beyond the fun office environment, we've increased benefits tremendously over the past five years. We offer competitive benefits and our employees have a role within a rising, international company with tremendous growth opportunities. Our entrepreneurial spirit allows employees to be involved in all aspects of the business.

We have evolved into a strategic organization that is guided by a strategic three-year plan that has helped all aspects of the business. We are focused on creating better, innovative products, reinventing stale product categories, global development, being number one in every product category, more automated distribution and logistics, and meeting the goals of our mission statement. Thanks to this plan, everybody is marching in the same direction. The most common goals take precedence over the little things that come up every day. Ultimately, our strategic plan helps keep things focused.

At the same time, we work in a marketplace that changes very rapidly; therefore, we need to have a business model that allows for quick response. If we realize that we need to make a change, our team has to be talented, strong and flexible enough to make that change while keeping our overall strategic plan in mind.

Our company's core values and principles include ensuring that we are handling business as ethically and professionally as possible. Everybody wants to work for an organization that always takes the right road; our reputation in the industry is based on those basic principles that were set early on in this organization. Our biggest core values include having integrity and honesty and showing each other respect. We do not have a corner office mentality; we are all peers and we all bring different strengths to the team.

A Unique Perspective: A "Start-Up" Mindset

One of the secrets of our company's success is that we retain a "start-up" mindset even though we are a big business. We are open to innovation, reward fresh thinking, and look to keep work fun. This philosophy has paid off in a big way in terms of the partnerships and products we have been able to create. For instance, we have a licensing partnership from The Disney Company to design, manufacture, and market toys for the Baby Einstein™ brand. Some of our newest introductions include the Baby Einstein Musical Motion Activity Jumper and the Color Kaleidoscope. Not what you traditionally picture when you hear "jumper," the Musical Motion Activity Jumper is an entertainer with a rotating seat and jumper all in one. The Color Kaleidoscope features dancing lights, melodies, and spoken color names in three languages that reward baby's curiosity through three stages of discovery as baby grows.

We also have a tremendous understanding of operations and logistics and how being successful in these areas can lead to huge strengths over our competitors. Our innovation goals do not just involve product development.

In order to reinvent ourselves over the past few years, we needed to create an "all hands on deck" mentality. Our goal was to create an international business, which has been growing at the rate of 100 percent a year. Since we are new in many of our markets, we have to meet the challenge of training new people and engaging in product testing and design in new countries and cultures. Since requirements vary by country, the greatest challenge is the multiple testing. It is hard to design products toward a common standard when country requirements vary. We must ensure that our products meet worldwide standards as well as market-by-market testing standards. The international side of our organization has what is similar to a '90s dot.com mentality, in that we are a very young, high energy organization that would like to reinvent this entire industry, from product design to manufacturing processes and account management.

Generating Revenues and Profits: The Importance of IP

Our financial focus is on building our proprietary brands, retaining and pursuing partnerships with premier brands, and looking internationally for rapid growth.

We seek to add value to our company through:

- A distribution infrastructure that is automated and offers improved forecasting and other efficiencies, including both direct and indirect shipment options ensuring that we are distributing our products in the most efficient, cost-effective manner to our customers, constantly making improvements and not resting on our laurels.
- Protected intellectual property (IP) of our products, brands, and designs on a global basis
- Developing people and constantly improving our product
- Strategic relationships
- Maximizing new technologies such as the Internet

Overall, IP—patents, trademarks, and brands—are some of our company's greatest assets. The better you develop these assets, the more valuable they become, just like our staff.

We have invested heavily in product development and brands over the last five years. In the past our focus was on low tech products. Our product line included a lot of sewn items such as bedding; obviously, our competition was great and there was not a lot of room for innovation. Today we are focusing heavily on electronics, plastics, and other higher ticket items; we are going into very mature categories and completely redefining them, increasing the need for IP protection.

We now spend a great deal on product and consumer research that includes ethnographic studies, in home testing, focus groups and online studies. We also tap into our Generation Mom network—an extensive product advisory group made up of hundreds of parents from around the world. The group provides product feedback, ideas, advice, and observations from their own playrooms, regarding fun (and not fun) activities for young children—and parents. These days, when we decide to launch a product it is because we have determined, through research, that it is a product that the consumer wants and needs. Thanks to this research, the effectiveness of our product launches has improved tremendously. We have launched eighty new items this year and less than four are struggling; this is a success ratio we have never had before.

An International Focus

Every year there are more similarities than differences between our U.S. operations and those in the global market because we have done a great job of finding out what those commonalities are and driving our products towards them. Ultimately, a mom's needs in the United States are not that different from the needs of a mom in Australia or the United Kingdom.

We are pushing that international focus in our total product development process, from manufacturing to distribution. We have gone from having six brands to just three brands that we are very focused on internationally. A few years ago we developed 120 to 140 new products a year; now we are down to launching seventy new items that will probably be more successful because we are more focused. The fewer SKUs you have, the easier it is to manage your business in all aspects, from promotion to operational management. This strategy has led to many helpful economies and efficiencies. For example, we created a global supply chain, invested heavily in an international infrastructure, and have cut our inventory substantially.

When we took Kids II international, we were able to go to our strategic partners such as Disney and say, "If you partner with us, you can deal with one company that covers the globe, versus dealing with a small organization that operates in a single country." We can help a company manage its brand in a consistent manner instead of dealing with multi-tiered partnerships. Kids II can provide consistency across the board to our partners. We make it easy for companies like Disney to achieve a consistent look, from product design to marketing. We're like a one-stop-shop because we bring our vendor relationships, retail partners, and distribution channels to the table as well as our internal resources. Our partners know they can entrust their brands with us both nationally and internationally. We bring a focused attitude to our marketing jobs. When we develop a strategic partnership, we put a cross-functional team on the project. We are able to go to vendors that specialize in certain areas and bring that worldwide distribution strength to them.

We have gone from calling on about 28,000 retail outlets directly to over 75,000; because there is no distributor or middleman, we manage the entire relationship with the retailer. We also control our brand building efforts globally in terms of our strategic partnerships with licensors, design firms, and vendors. Ultimately, leveraging our infrastructure continues to provide growing revenue and business opportunities.

Product Launches and Research and Development

Our business requires constant innovation. We launch new products annually—in this industry, you have to keep your product line fresh. Our team of product development experts works year round to innovate or update products. Only a small percentage of ideas make it through the vetting process and we put all products through extensive third-party testing against all standards for each country. We have a strong track record of success with examples of award-winning products across all categories from toys to play gyms to entertainers and bath items. For instance, the Bright Starts™ Around We Go! ™ was one of the top-selling SKUs at Babies R Us for the 2005 holiday season. It's not the category but the toy itself that made it successful. In terms of testing, we conduct testing throughout the development process including concept and design research, prototype review and evaluation, safety testing and analysis in all stages of product development, final product testing, consumer use studies (pre launch). In addition, after a product has launched, we continue with post evaluation studies.

We work on product cycles and have a very detailed, continual eighteen-month development plan. Product lifecycles are relatively short in the toy industry—about one to two years—so we need to stay ahead of the industry and our competitors. We also have a team working specifically on projects that are eighteen months plus. Larger, more complex products and those involving innovations tend to take a little longer in the pipeline. We always stay flexible and try to adjust to the latest market trends because trends in this industry change fast.

Feedback is a vital part of any product launch. We listen to our advisory panel of moms and also get input from some of the most experienced infant product developers in the industry. Also, our retail partners, such as Wal-Mart and Target, are very tapped into the latest insights of their shoppers, and they share those insights with us.

In addition, we conduct a monthly innovation meeting that encourages attendees to bring ideas from across the globe back to our Atlanta headquarters. We then track those ideas from start to finish. Product is not the only topic in these innovation meetings. Operations, logistics, system improvements, and other topics factor into the innovation mix. We cull the best ideas and update our strategic plans regularly.

The Role of the Toy Industry CEO

Sales, Marketing, Product Development

As CEO of a major toy company, the three departments that are most important to me are:

Sales: This is a very difficult department to manage in today's business world. One must be savvy in many areas of business in order to manage our accounts. Old school sales philosophies just do not work a good amount of the time. Sales involve a lot more business management skills. The "sell-in" process is very analytical and we offer a complete service to our retail partners making it more complex. I like to see our teams plan ahead and drive sales within all areas and levels of the business by forecasting, managing in-stocks, monitoring account profitability, margin requirements, and constantly examining the marketplace to identify successful and unsuccessful SKUs so we can quickly adjust to meet the marketplace needs.

Marketing: Marketing successfully involves making sure we are managing with real-time information. Staying on top of the business in terms of retail and product marketing, as well as managing our brands, and being aware of how this process applies to the global market, is a major challenge. Our key marketing managers must have the mentality that they are presidents of their own companies, in terms of what brand they handle. They must own and drive that company within our agreed upon strategies, or drive consensus for new thinking. Motivation is the key to success.

Product development: Understanding the investment required to gain true innovation is sometimes a challenge; analyzing the return on this investment is a greater challenge. We explore how our Product Development Group can drive innovation through outside relationships. We sometimes get caught up with thinking that we need to do the whole job ourselves, when many times we can move exponentially faster if we use outside relationships with vendors, outside designers, and so on. Delivering product innovation and increasing speed annually is the key to success in this area.

Creating a Winning Team

Talent, passion, and the ability to laugh are qualities I look for when choosing key staff members at Kids II because toy manufacturing is a fun industry. Loyalty to the business and an ownership mentality are also key character traits for our employees. Anyone on our team must bring a skill set that offsets the weaknesses of others in the organization, including my own.

Whenever I conduct meetings I am likely to spend ten minutes talking about matters extraneous to the meeting topic. Sometimes new people think it is a bit weird, but it is a great way for me to get in touch with the people who work for my organization, and it breaks down a lot of barriers that are traditional in other businesses. We have a lot of designers in our organization and the entire environment at our company is structured to fuel the creativity process. I believe when workers feel relaxed, inspired and motivated, it fuels productivity. Some old school people may think some of our people play Ping-Pong too much, but you have to have the mindset that playing Ping-Pong is an outlet for these staff members, and they will be a lot more productive once they get back down to work. A person who is engaged with his or her work has a different, more creative mentality and I think nurturing that mentality is the new wave of today's business environment.

Successful Strategies

The three strategies that have helped make me a successful CEO in this industry include continually developing my key people through growth opportunities, listening well and reacting rapidly, and increasing my intense focus on global strategies. I am leading our international expansion, which represents huge growth opportunities for us. I have created partnerships with some of the premier brands in the business, from Disney to Baby Einstein™ to Boppy®. I have also recruited and retained some of the top talent in this industry.

At the end of the day, with the right people and products, our potential is limitless. Additional strategies include removing the middleman in our international offices to improve speed of response and communication, continuing our heavy investment in IP over the past four years, which is really paying off, and developing an Asian logistics and base;. China is a huge market with long-term potential. Other key markets include Singapore, Hong Kong, Korea, Taiwan, and Japan.

Overcoming Challenges

The challenging aspects of being a CEO in the toys and games industry are probably similar to other industries. We need to recruit and retain top talent, we need to constantly push for innovation, and we need to stay on top of the numbers. In our case, we must also deliver exceptional service to our customers, globally. We stay in touch with our accounts, personally, and in the process, we come to understand the environment and problems unique to each account, communicate their goals and objectives to our organization, and set them up to win.

This is a fast-paced industry; therefore, we have to meet the challenges involved with anticipating the future and setting strategy. Our industry also requires a lot of contingency planning. We always try to understand the faults in our strategy setting and are ready to hear alternative perspectives. If one person thinks something is wrong, 1,000 other people probably think the same way.

Probably the biggest misconception about being a CEO in our industry is that it is all fun and games. Of course, we are running a business too. The most difficult situations I am faced with in my position as CEO are selling and communicating our vision, and constantly evaluating our business model to make sure we continue to stay relevant.

In our industry we deal with multiple opinions and personalities; we have the mindset that we are peers and that everybody's voice is equally important. However, not everyone at every time will buy into the same overall strategy, so it can be a challenge to reach a balance between letting everybody have their say and being the one to make the final decision. Ultimately, the CEO's job is to set the vision for your company and get everyone to buy into it.

Today, our company is twelve times the size of when I first started with the organization. We had one office five years ago; today we have nine. During this period of growth it has been a challenge to maintain our culture and vision as we change and evolve. It has also been a huge challenge to make sure we are communicating that vision to nine different offices. Our Atlanta office is now our corporate headquarters, where we do our planning and strategy setting. Our goal is to do 80 percent of our planning here and let our regional offices manage and execute the rest of the process such as guiding the plan to fit their local retailers' needs, setting their retailers up for success, and overall helping their customers win because then we win.

Evaluating your company's business model is another major challenge; you have to make sure you continue to be relevant to your customers and to your vendor and design communities. You need to understand the business models of your competitors in order to make sure your long-term vision is set up to be successful. If you are not aware of what is going on out in the business environment and are not adaptive, then you become stale. Your executive team must have a mindset that is able to set new goals and learn from its mistakes; it needs to be able to react to everything that is thrown at it and find ways to take advantage of whatever opportunities come its way. It all comes down to assembling a great team of people; it is very rewarding when you get everybody firing at all cylinders and pulling in the same direction.

Almost every organization goes through a period where there are lulls—you are not as relevant, you are facing tough competitive forces, or you are a little stale on IP. When that happens, you have to be able to tough it out and try to reinvent yourself, or adapt to the situation in a very smart way.

Keys to Success: Helpful Advice

I see the key to my long-term success as being able to retain our top talent, as well as my passion for the category and ongoing innovation within it. Part of developing a successful strategy is having the buy-in of your creative team. I want them to help set our strategy and be a part of it. If they develop a strategy, they are much more likely to buy into it. This is all part of the process of developing people and giving them the bandwidth needed to grow professionally.

I always advise my team members to focus, listen, and move fast. I tell them that teamwork is a key ingredient to a company's success; it is important to manage healthy conflict and stay positive. I also tell my team members to continually visualize where the competition is going, and apply this to our strategy on where we plan to go.

A key question I ask in every staff meeting is, "How does this decision apply to our international business?" It gets everyone to think globally. I also tell them to come to meetings with alternatives, not just problems. In theory, we as executives work for our staff; they do not work for us. We must be accountable to the entire organization.

The best piece of advice I have ever received from another CEO is to respect and listen to other opinions, even if they differ from yours. It is good to hear alternative opinions because you can always learn from them, even if you choose not to follow them.

If I were to advise another CEO in this industry, I would tell him or her to develop a long-term vision and pursue it relentlessly. It is important to hire the right people and empower them to get the job done. It is equally important to keep an eye and ear on the industry, because it is competitive and fast-paced—and set up an environment at your company that can keep up with that pace.

Keeping Your Edge

Constant analysis of the competition and predicting what their next moves will be are key to maintaining success in this industry, as well as developing a deep understanding of retail dynamics. Therefore, it is important to keep your edge. I read a lot while traveling in order to keep up to speed on what is going on in the industry. I am always looking for new ideas and when I read an article, I always ask myself how the information it contains applies to Kids II and can help us stay relevant.

I love talking to other CEOs and executives in order to seek information about challenges I am facing. Bouncing ideas off of friends and colleagues in a relaxed atmosphere is a great way to get feedback and serves as a continuous learning process. What you know today quite possibly may not be true tomorrow, so it is important to maintain a constant flow of information.

When you travel to different markets and get in front of the customers you come to understand the problems faced by different retailers in different countries—and you need to consider how you can help retailers solve these problems. If we find something that works in one market, we try to standardize it and suggest it to other markets, because quite possibly those solutions are worldwide. Retailers are often very eager to hear about successful merchandising practices in other markets and how Kids II can serve them and hopefully make them more successful. Therefore, staying connected on the customer front in terms of serving their needs is vital; making our customers successful adds revenue for us.

A Changing Role

The role of toy industry CEO, and the industry itself, have undergone significant changes in the past few years. For instance, there are fewer retailers in the United States and more multinational retailers needing global service. Another big change is the intense pressure to innovate or die. Retailers will bypass your organization if you do not add value.

In the years to come, I anticipate that more flexible distribution systems will service customers, reducing retailer inventories and continuing to maximize sales. The global business environment and the process of gaining new economies will fundamentally impact operations. Increasingly, operational excellence will drive success or failure.

Golden Rules

My three golden rules of being a CEO in the toys and games industry are to keep focus, keep moving forward, and keep it fun.

If you want to keep your company moving forward, you have to focus on a goal and have a healthy dissatisfaction with the status quo. I am always looking for the next great thing; it is good to celebrate your successes, but you have to keep moving forward or someone else will pass you by. In other words, keep moving or you will become stale. You also have to try to win more than you lose.

At our company, we enjoy going to work. Not every day is a great day, but the majority of our days are. It is a challenge to keep that kind of fun-filled environment ongoing, but if you can, it is very rewarding.

Ryan Gunnigle, Kids II president and chief executive officer, believes innovation in baby products comes from understanding the gap between moms' needs and what's in the marketplace. As a father of two, Mr. Gunnigle knows the trials and tribulations of new mommies and daddies, but more importantly understands the value of enjoying the everyday fun of parenting. Innovating fun for parent and child is his mission at Kids II, which he joined in 1989 as associate product manager.

President since 1998 and named president and chief executive officer in 2005, Mr. Gunnigle introduced the company to global expansion, successful licensing partnerships including Boppy®, Baby Einstein,™ and Winnie the Pooh, and gained a ranking as one of Atlanta's Top 100 Private Companies. A graduate of Emory University, Mr. Gunnigle's newest innovations have been supporting the reintroduction of Bright Starts,™ the company's flagship brand, and the company's European/international launch.

Dedication: *Dedicated to Tom Gunnigle, my father.*

Putting the Fun in Play

Neil Friedman

President, Mattel Brands

Mattel, Inc.

Play. It's the word that describes everything we do and all that we are at Mattel. While the ultimate goal of any toy manufacturer is to bring innovative products to market that engage and delight children, Mattel leads the industry in its ability to build global brands. We are the leading maker of toys in the world with such household names as Barbie®, Hot Wheels®, Fisher-Price®, and American Girl®. The other barometer for success is the extent to which our brand penetrates into adjacent areas, such as apparel, home décor, entertainment, electronics, and sporting goods, to name a few. To be successful, our brands, not just our toys, need to be where kids are today.

But sales are just one measure of our success—being a good corporate citizen and contributing to the communities where we employee and operate is another important measure at Mattel. As the first and the only in the toy industry to commit to independent monitoring and public reporting of our factories, Mattel's dedication to ethical manufacturing has been a leading factor in the current transparency efforts in the toy industry and beyond.

We keep measure of our success by utilizing third parties' research organizations that work directly with retailers. By analyzing their data, we are able to gain a comprehensive overview of product movement and consumer behavior that allows us to stay up to date on where we are doing well and where we need to make adjustments.

Our vision for the company is to be the world's premier toy company for today and tomorrow. Simply put, we strive to be leaders in sales and trends where we compete on a global basis.

Unique Marketing Challenges

Achieving success in the toy manufacturing industry offers unique challenges as the primary consumer for your products is a very young child—the most fickle consumer possible, with the shortest attention span. To appeal to that consumer base, it's crucial to be ahead of trends as the toy industry operates much like the fashion or cosmetic industry. It is a constantly changing business because your consumer base is constantly evolving.

To maintain our leading edge in a very competitive and fast-moving environment, we engage in observational research, which involves children, parents, and grandparents. We believe no other children's products organization does more consumer research than Mattel through the utilization of focus groups, quantitative studies, in-home research, Internet surveys, and our on-site Playlabs. By simply studying everyday occurrences and observing behaviors among our smallest consumers, we can identify opportunities to create new products or improve existing ones to help enhance the value—and fun—of play

Successful Strategies

It actually sounds pretty simple—bring great toys to market and you will be successful. But satisfying a very young and finicky consumer is challenging work. The key to creating innovative products is in maintaining the balance between trend, technology, material, and function, all to exemplify timeless play patterns and learning stages. And we approach this balancing act rather differently from other toy companies as we obtain great ideas from internal and external sources. We work with a wide range of external inventors with vast expertise. Whether ideas are generated internally or externally does not matter as long as they fit within the scope of our business.

At Mattel, we work hard to turn good ideas into great products. That is the foundation of our competitive edge, made even stronger by time-tested expertise in bringing those ideas and products to market better than any other company in the industry. It is important to note that toy companies are not typically leading-edge suppliers of technology, but rather they take trailing-edge technology and make it applicable to younger children and associated play patterns.

The cultivation of these key relationships with external inventors, product engineers, and designers ensures that many come to Mattel with their new ideas or concepts. From those initial meetings, our internal design teams are able to identify current or future products or brands that may benefit from an added technology or feature.

Building and maintaining a successful company structure involves identifying the best and most talented people for each and every discipline of your business—giving them the opportunity to execute their plans successfully, allowing them the opportunity to be creative, and making sure they, in turn, train and coach their teams. Ultimately, we all have to work together in order to execute successful product development, production, and marketing plans; everyone on the team, whatever their task, must be focused on the same objectives in order to achieve success.

Building a Winning Team

At Mattel, we value play. To be the foundation of an organization's culture, common values cannot be created, they can only be discovered. Mattel's corporate values are based on a grassroots effort by Mattel employees to meld our core competency—play—into our values statement. And our values resonate strongly with employees, as well as with our industry. To summarize, Mattel's values statement says we must "play with passion" by infusing unparalleled creativity and innovation into every aspect of work, loving what we do, and having the courage to make a difference. We must "play together" through dynamic teamwork and collaboration. We must "play fair" by treating others with dignity and respect, and acting with integrity each and every day. And we must "play to grow" by seeking continuous improvements in the business and rewarding excellence. Leaders at Mattel align themselves with our core values in a way that motivates and inspires others to take action. Our values set the tone for the manner in which we accomplish our work and inspire employees to always strive to go beyond expectations.

The attributes required for success in the toy industry include discipline, creativity, and the ability to execute ideas, as well as intelligence, imagination, energy, and enthusiasm. And it doesn't hurt to be able to identify with your inner child as well!

No matter the industry, no leader can go it alone. My closest contacts at the company include the general managers of our various divisions, brand finance and operations, media, entertainment and licensing, and other corporate executives. While a toy begins with a great idea or an innovative use of technology, a variety of departments and people touch a toy in its life cycle from ideation to store shelf. The toy must be carefully designed and engineered, materials must be identified and sourced, costs must be calculated—and that's all before it even hits the production line. In order for our relationship to be successful and profitable, my general managers must understand what I expect from them and need for them to do. They have to execute projects on schedule and allow their people the space to be creative and thoughtful, as well as develop their own leadership skills. The most successful and effective leaders at Mattel must have a thorough understanding of the marketplace, our consumers and the industry, and maintain a sound relationship with the sales force and with the retail community.

Launching a Product

The two major windows of opportunity for retailers are the spring and fall sales seasons, which are when new products hit store shelves. Toy companies must be ready to launch products within those two major timeframes. Our product development cycle can be anywhere from eighteen months to two and a half years, depending on what the product is, the complexity, and what technology is involved in producing it. We can—and sometimes do—introduce a product in just six months if we see a trend emerge, but generally, unless the product is very unique, we like to see if it stands the test of time. To capture a very specific or possibly short-lived trend, we would move the development cycle up. There is not one class of product that takes longer per say but, for example, technology-driven toys could take longer because they are much more complicated to manufacture that a basic Hot Wheels® car or Barbie® doll.

Before launching any product, it is essential to understand the dynamics of the marketplace; if you do not, chances are the product will not fit with consumer demand. In addition to the vast consumer research Mattel undertakes, we also conduct retail research to find out what our customers are looking for, based on consumer demand. We combine all of this knowledge, then look at the marketplace, note the latest trends, and see how all of it fits together. It is a very complicated process, but one that is attainable with the right people and the right skills. Ultimately, decisions for which products make it to market are made by the general managers of each business unit in conjunction with the head of sales.

Increasing Sales

Mattel's strategy for increasing sales in any of our divisions is to first bring great products to market then follow up with great integrated marketing campaigns, which include a variety of communication touch points including publicity, promotions, Internet, and television advertising. This simple strategy drives our business and builds our brands.

At Mattel, we have a formalized review process that holds employees and teams accountable to measurable goals but the goals come from the top. At the beginning of the year, the company issues to its employees worldwide the year's priorities and goals for the year. Employees are expected to integrate Mattel's objectives into their personal goals so that everyone in the company, regardless of department, is aligned and focused on singular objectives.

Challenges Facing a Leader

The biggest challenge for the toy industry executive is finding and hiring great people and keeping them for a long period of time—the longer a team works together, the better the team gets. Keeping a senior executive team and/or a design marketing and sales team together over a long period of time is a very big challenge in any industry; being able to do just that has contributed a great deal to our company's success. We recruit talent from some of the top design and business schools in New York and Los Angeles. We also have a very extensive internship program that enables us to groom talent students in a variety of functional areas.

Employees tend to stay with our company because we offer them a lot of creative leeway, along with a high level of responsibility and accountability. That kind of atmosphere makes people want to stay, learn more, and go on to the next level; we promote from within very heavily. Employees can trust that Mattel stands behind integrity. It's not just what we achieve, but how we achieve success that is important. Conducting business with integrity builds trust with employees, and our employees can be proud that they work for a company that stands for doing what is right.

Common Misconceptions

The most common misconception about heading up a toy company is that it is an easy job. It is actually a very challenging position, because we have to reinvent ourselves every year. We may have the same brands, but usually more than 80 percent of our product line changes annually. We run an enormous business just utilizing our base brands; our product base is probably bigger than any other toy company if you factor in the volume of new products that are added on a year-to-year basis.

The Changing Role of a Leader

The toy industry is always changing and evolving. There are fewer toy retailers, but many new channels of distribution, including alternative channels like grocery and drug stores, as well as Web sites. In order to keep my edge in the industry, I have to stay on top of the latest product research and trends, and stay heavily involved in the creation of our products.

There is also the issue of age compression—the phenomenon of children getting older younger. Contrary to the long held belie, age compression does not affect all toy companies equally, as toy companies that cater to an older age group have more reason to be concerned. While age compression is certainly on our radar screen, Mattel is focusing its energies on targeting the growing consumer segment that is playing with toys, rather than chasing a group that is maturing beyond traditional toys.

Every year poses new challenges, from finding new ways to properly price products due to the rising prices of inputs to reinventing your brands based on new competition and other happenings in the marketplace. Those challenges change every year; the only thing that is consistent in our industry is change, and you have to be able to evolve with it.

Achieving Long-Term Success

The best advice I can give to any toy industry executive is to hire the smartest people you can find in each discipline; and to hire the most creative people to develop your products. We are dealing with imagination, creativity, and the needs of a child.

The successful leader in this industry needs to be passionate and also able to inspire and motivate employees, while imparting the direction they need to take in order to successfully execute. The key to success is to surround yourself with great people and teach them how to replace you when necessary; all higher level employees need to train those who work under them effectively, so that when they are promoted they have a trained successor in place and are ready to hit the ground running. This process gives high potential talent at Mattel an opportunity for growth and reinforces the idea that they are valued for what they do; it also provides a clear and distinct direction for everyone to follow.

The three golden rules of being a successful president in the toy industry: focus, imagination, and execution. When you have that, you are ready to play!

A visionary who first helped popularize the pairing of technology and toys, Toy Industry Hall of Famer Neil Friedman is president of the Mattel Brands division at Mattel Inc., which includes the Barbie®, Hot Wheels® and Fisher-Price® toy products, Mattel Games, and licensed entertainment properties, such as toys for Batman®, Dora the Explorer™, and Sesame Street®.

Among his many industry accomplishments, Mr. Friedman is credited with the huge success of Tickle Me Elmo, one of the first mainstream toy hits to incorporate technology to enhance traditional preschool play. As president of Fisher-Price Brands from 1999 to 2005, he oversaw the successful introduction of electronic learning toys that increased the core Fisher-Price business. Today, kids expect technology to be an integral part of their daily lives, and their toys.

Mr. Friedman joined Mattel in March 1997, following the merger between Tyco Toys Inc. and Mattel. Prior to joining Tyco Preschool in 1995, he served as president of MCA/Universal Merchandising; senior vice president, marketing and operations, Just Toys; general manager, baby care division, Gerber Products; president, Aviva/Hasbro, Hasbro's import division; and executive vice president and chief operating officer of Lionel Leisure/Kiddie City.

In February 2004, Mr. Friedman was inducted into the prestigious Toy Industry Hall of Fame by the Toy Industry Association. Mr. Friedman currently serves as chairman of the Toy Industry Foundation board of trustees, the charitable arm of the association, where he also serves as an advisory member to the organization's board of directors. He also is a past chairman of the Licensing Industry Merchandisers' Association and an advisor to the board.

In 2001, Mr. Friedman received the prestigious Marco Polo Award from the U.S.-China Foundation for the role Mattel and Fisher-Price have played in China's economic development and for the improvement of Chinese society. Previous winners of the Marco Polo Award include President George Bush.

Mr. Friedman attended Rider University in Lawrenceville, New Jersey, where he majored in finance. He serves on the boards of several charitable organizations, including the executive advisory board of Children Affected by AIDS Foundation and the Northside Center for Child Development (New York, New York).

Dedication: To Kevin Curran, general manager of Fisher-Price.

Building to Succeed in the Toy and Game Industry

Joel Glickman

Founder, Chairman, and Chief Executive Officer

K'NEX Industries, Inc.

Corporate Goals

The goals of a chief executive officer (CEO) in the toys and games industry, and my goals in particular, are primarily strategic in nature. In the case of our company, our specific goals include:

- Capturing 25 percent of the global construction toy market in the next three to five years
- Developing a brand vision that is a base for the next thirty years of K'NEX
- Fulfilling our brand promise: "Imagine – Build – Play"
- Exceeding our customers' expectations
- Making sure K'NEX employees are people with the best talent and a winning attitude

In a sense, we do structure our goals and our approach to them on a "checks and balances" system, but we find that the "balance" of the organization will occur as a matter of routine once we have great experts in their disciplines. We are also fortunate to have great financial reporting and internal controls, sophisticated information technology systems, the best of breed warehousing capabilities, and fabulous designers. We have in place an enormously talented sales and marketing team that drive our brand recognition and generate our income. During my years in this role, I have found that when you align the entire company around the sales and marketing efforts and let the experts give you their best advice, a successful balance is the natural result of your team's efforts.

The Toy and Games Industry

While I do not know exactly what it is like to run other companies in every other industry, I can confidently surmise that we have a lot more fun running our company than most corporate executives do. The toy and games industry is a creative, dynamic field that enables us to truly embrace and enjoy what we do.

There are certain unique elements of the toy industry. For example, much of the industry is focused on "hot" trends or tied to movie releases, which is always a creative, time-sensitive endeavor. Also, unlike most industries, most of the manufacturers are managing global supply chains that tie in some way to Asia in general, and usually China in particular. One unique challenge to this industry is that it is rare to find a brand that has any real staying power for more than three years. Further, there is pressure for toys and games to stay relevant in an increasingly electronic/computerized world.

In running K'NEX, we are lucky in the following respects:

1. Construction toys are a staple within the industry. All children go through a stage of manipulative development. This is actually just a fancy way of saying they have to learn how to use their hands in a coordinated way.

2. Our product line starts at age three (with KID K'NEX) and has no intellectual ceiling. Most of our customers stop using K'NEX at age fourteen, although it is part of the curriculum in high schools and universities around the world.

3. Parents like to buy construction toys because they know that they are tools with which children learn the basics of math, physics, and physical science through open-ended play.

4. We have a brand that is entering its fifteenth year, which means we have earned the trust of millions of people over the years. We stand for quality and play value, and our customers know it. It also means that we now have parents who played with K'NEX as children buying the product for their children.

5. We distribute BRIO toys exclusively in the United States and Canada. That brand is over 150 years old, and is also known for quality and excellent play value.

6. We distribute Lincoln Logs exclusively in the United States and Canada. This brand is also over ninety years old; it has tremendous nostalgic appeal, and is still made of 100 percent wooden logs.

7. We have developed an expertise in mastering the global supply chain, as well as fulfilling orders for customers in over twenty countries.

These elements of stability offset the highly dynamic and ever-changing nature of the toy industry as a whole, while allowing us to enjoy many of the other unique elements of the industry, such as the creative and educational components of our business.

Our company's approach to the toys and games business is different than the approach of many other companies in this industry. We do not worry much about what our competitors may or may not be doing. We make sure we keep our entrepreneurial spirit, a winning attitude, and relentless pursuit of innovative product, which leads to a great team effort. Simply put, we walk tall and dream loud.

Developing a Leadership Plan: A Corporate Vision Designed for Success

Our leadership plan centers around three core principles:

1. *Being customer-centric:* This means evaluating every decision we make in the business from the perspective of our customers. In our business we have two main categories of customers: retailers and kids. In order to make the kids happy, we have to put out cool products with which they can have success. We define a kid's success as an enjoyable building experience, and an enjoyable playing experience after the build. An example would be a child who builds a really cool roller coaster and is able to enjoy it running properly for hours after he or she built it. With respect to retailers, the main focus is on SKU productivity. In many respects, we manage the inventory of our customers. The better we do at that, the more shelf space we get, and the greater return on investment we both experience.

2. *Being true to our brand promise:* Our brand promise is in our tag line, which is "Imagine – Build – Play." It means that with our construction system, a child can literally build anything that he or she can imagine, and it will move just like the real thing. Recently, we donated over 100,000 parts to an eleven-year-old in Colorado who wanted to build a scale model of the Golden Gate Bridge. When he was finished, it was 160' long and 24' high and was an exact 1/40th scale model of the original. From a car to a roller coaster to a ten-story building, our product has to live up to this promise.

3. *Setting the financial targets:* Ultimately, the business has to be profitable consistently to continue to thrive. In order to achieve this, our senior management team sets the budget. My role is to set the short, medium and long-term goals. As our company marches towards owning 25 percent of the construction toy market, it is imperative to set and attain financial targets. I have my eye on 50 percent, but I will be patient in striving for that (although some have suggested I may be growing impatient!).

The Importance of Client Service

Client service is the key to continuing business. While we do have a customer service department, it is imperative for every employee—not just those working in that department—to understand that customer service is implicit in everything we do.

We incorporate market/client feedback through a variety of methods. We use focus groups, online surveys, and monitoring of trends that are important to us. For example, we test all our instructions with kids in focus groups to make sure the instructions are clear and age appropriate. In addition, we have kids test new concepts right in our design department, so that K'NEX designers can see exactly how kids respond to the ideas. We also ask kids who visit our Web site to answer short surveys about trends and other topics. We subscribe to trade journals and watch and read kid media to stay current with what interests kids.

Ensuring Your Company Generates Growing Revenues and Profits

The two main benchmarks our company uses to measure success are inventory turns and market share. Inventory turns refer to a measure of how long it takes to sell through a specific quantity of inventory. Market share is the percent of market sales attributed to an individual brand of company; share is generally measured in either dollars or units. To achieve success and generate growing revenues, the single most important element of a business is hiring and retaining stellar employees. Accordingly, we seek out and retain the best people in their respective fields. The simple truth is that without great people, we would not be the success we are today, nor could we grow in the ways we have planned. We also control our own manufacturing, distribution, sales, marketing, and research and development. By controlling these key aspects of our business, we continually upgrade our efficiencies and develop expertise in delivering goods to our retail partners when they need them. The most important thing I do that has a direct financial impact on my company is to focus on the importance of teamwork. I am sure if it was just me we would not be where we are today. I hope I motivate our people to stay true to our brand vision and promise. I make efforts to stay customer centric and keep carrying that message to our team. I believe by continually sharing the vision we have created together with each other, we are bound to succeed.

This strategy, coupled with a stellar execution, helps us take away market share from competitors because ultimately, the best product wins.

How Pricing Works in This Industry

There are some key driving price points in our segment of the industry. After all, people buy toys mainly for birthdays and holidays. So, we need to determine the right combination of value and ____ Our approach is to over deliver on the value at every price ____

The spectrum of prices that ____ products and services ranges from $1.99 to $199.99 ____ pricing has some impact on our pricing strategies ____ process is a reality check against what our competition ____ similar price points. In addition, we work closely with reta____ make sure the products are promoted in their best promotional vehicles at attractive pricing.

pricing process is a reality check against competition.

While I cannot share the details of our confidential research and development program, I can tell you we launch new products every year, and the line is totally refreshed on an average of every three years. In many ways, the toy industry is like the fashion industry, albeit with fewer seasons. As such, we are constantly in development of new products.

The CEO's Team

I personally work most closely with our president and chief operating officer, and our vice president of product design. Our chief operating officer handles the day-to-day operations, freeing me to focus on the items I have outlined above. Because I am in the unique position of being the inventor of the product and founder of the company, and because I love making K'NEX better every year, I spend a great deal of time with our talented design team. Cooperation and success are easy if I get the unfiltered news. There is no such thing as good news or bad news—there is just news. When armed with the facts, we can make a decision; without them, we are lost.

Each team member has a vital role in this company. In terms of driving revenue and ensuring customer satisfaction, for K'NEX, it all comes back to sales and marketing. We focus on having a coordinated brand message and great value proposition across our entire product line. The other two critical areas are product development and operations. The coordination of these three groups is the linchpin of our success. After all, without amazing K'NEX builds that function really well, and without delivering the product when our retailers need it, our sales and marketing efforts would be severely hampered.

The skills that are most important to me in members of my team include integrity, a passion for winning, and an unwillingness to take no for an answer. Employees who work at our company must thrive on growth and possess a great ability to make risk assessments even when facing imperfect or incomplete information.

Strategies as a CEO

My overall strategies include staying focused on growing the business, maintaining total visibility to my sales, costs, and supply chain, making my customers successful, and over-delivering in quality and value for consumers.

My personal strategy, and one that has served me well professionally, is to "Walk Tall and Dream Loud." This means developing the confidence of all of our people in the decisions they make every day. By picking talented people in the first place, and then developing their knowledge base, our competitive advantage grows every day. Our company is not unique in that we deal with many people outside of our buildings. Projecting confidence, especially when backed by the facts and performance, means our relationships with our customers, vendors, and suppliers are more productive. It also means focusing part of each employee's day on the possibilities for growth. I have seen too many managers over the years attach built-in assumptions for the size of a market or a growth plan or a sales strategy. When a person puts limitations on their ideas, the maximum potential is limited. Because we do not do that, our growth potential is limitless. That does not mean it happens all in a day, but it does mean when we make a plan, it is for the next thirty years, and not just for the next thirty minutes.

Qualities of a CEO

First and foremost, any CEO must possess integrity and be honest in all his or her dealings with people. Secondly, it is helpful to have a good ability to analyze talent, both of people and technology. Thirdly, a CEO must understand what drives the success of his or her customers, and, upon understanding this, make sure the business makes its customers more successful. I think another important quality for any CEO to have is a love for the job: for example, there are many challenges in this industry, but they do not present a roadblock for me because I am having too much fun with my work to notice or worry about them.

Another critical element for any successful CEO is the ability to stay on top of emerging knowledge in his respective industry. I do this by making sure our senior management team has all the tools they need to perform at an optimal level. My senior management team each stays on top of their respective specialty, which they in turn highlight for me. I also confer regularly with other business leaders. I also regularly read various trade publications and Web resources, such as electronic industry newsletters and alerts from search engines.

Best Advice, Given and Received

When I am guiding or advising my team, I tell them to ask themselves: "How is what you are doing helping our customers?" Keeping this question—and its answer—in mind at all times ensures that employees are acting in a customer-driven manner that will bring satisfaction to our clients and positively represent our company. In turn, the best advice I have ever received from another CEO is: "The wise man knows what he does not know." This is a reason for making sure K'NEX identifies and retains the most talented people in their respective areas of expertise. It also reminds me to keep asking questions, even when I think I know the answer.

I believe there are basic "golden rules" of business that apply whether you are a CEO or not in any industry.

They are to:

- Treat everyone the way you want to be treated.
- Deal with your customers, suppliers, and vendors with integrity and honesty. Your reputation is all you have.
- "Walk Tall and Dream Loud."

While I would never presume to tell another CEO how to create his or her own vision, I do know what has worked for me and my company. If any of these philosophies, strategies, and tactics can be helpful to other CEOs, I am pleased to be able to share them.

Changes to the Toy and Games Industry

Over the past five years, my role has not changed much, but the industry itself has seen some changes. Over the last five years, the toy and games industry has become more concentrated in fewer retail customers. The specialty toy industry has declined and more consumers are shopping online.

Over the next few years, I do not expect my role as CEO or the toys and games industry to change significantly. Some time over the next decade, however, there will be a notable change in that both China and India will be sustainable markets into which we can sell.

Joel Glickman is founder, chairman of the board, and chief executive officer of K'NEX Industries Inc., including its Rodon division, one of the nation's largest privately held plastic injection-molding companies. He joined the family-owned Rodon Group in 1964, became president in 1966, and was named chief executive officer in 1975.

Mr. Glickman was instrumental in helping the Rodon Group grow from a small operation with four injection molding presses to a significant manufacturer of small injection molded plastic parts with more than 100 presses. Rodon serves more than 1,000 customers. Over the course of his more than forty years with the Rodon Group, Mr. Glickman has been granted fourteen patents.

In 1990, utilizing his years of experience in the plastic industry and his creative and design skills, Mr. Glickman conceived the original idea for K'NEX, an innovative and unique building system that hit the toy market in late 1992. Under Mr. Glickman's leadership, K'NEX has grown into a company with international distribution and one that is a major factor in the construction toy industry. The Rodon Group was merged into K'NEX Industries in 1999.

Mr. Glickman holds a bachelor of fine arts degree from Syracuse University.

Focusing on the Toy and Game Customer

Joe Hauck

Executive Vice President,
Sales, Marketing, and Product Development
WizKids Games

The Goals of the Position

As the executive vice president of sales, marketing, and product development at WizKids, it is my goal to integrate all aspects affecting the consumer experience together. In this industry, companies often rely too heavily on research and development without a real understanding of what the consumer really wants: ongoing and innovative game play with an intellectual property or theme that resonates with who they are. Often, companies attempt to sell derivative products without innovation by relying on heavy advertising, which may work in the short term but does not produce long-term success. My job is to balance these different approaches and to ensure that as a company, we create products that consumers have passion for, products that are placed where consumers ordinarily shop, and products that are priced at the optimal price. In addition, it is my job to make sure the consumer is aware of these products in the most cost-effective manner possible.

A System of Checks and Balances

Our company has recently gone through a change in executive management. A new approach is being used where market research is utilized and valued to provide clear direction to achieving our above goals. As we work as a team to instill this mind-set within the organization, we will be increasing a system of checks and balances in which we track consumers and retailers to determine if we are executing these goals appropriately. Our company, along with other collectible game companies, is in the position to see how well our approach is working. If we are doing our jobs correctly, we run out of a limited edition print run. When that happens, there is a lot of activity that shows up on what we call the secondary market. If players and collectors are happy, there is activity. If not, then our original plan was flawed in some manner and we have to go in and forensically determine what we did that was suboptimal for the consumer experience. This requires us to go back out and talk directly to the consumer as well as monitor their discussions on forums for our products. By engaging the consumer in conversations regarding our products and analyzing their behavioral responses to our new product offerings, we are able to better understand the minds of our consumers and make better decisions on future products and services.

Is the Toy and Game Business Different from Other Product-Oriented Businesses?

Ultimately, I believe the toys and games business is a consumer products type business, just like any other consumer products business. As an executive in the business, I haven't seen much evidence that the business is vastly different. We are still bound by the four Ps of marketing as every other packaged goods business: product, placement, pricing, and promotions. This being said, I will admit to certain idiosyncrasies that appear in our industry creating challenges that not all other packaged goods may experience.

First, it is important to understand that we are an entertainment product in addition to being a packaged good. Our competition is other forms of entertainment such as movies, television, the Internet, sports, and electronic games, and while they are all fun, none are necessities. Not only do we fight for shelf space from our toy and game competitors, we also compete for time share with these other forms of entertainment. This does require us to provide value on multiple dimensions in order to succeed both on the shelf at retail and within the lives of our consumers. Consumers find value in our products if our games provide them with repeat entertainment. Unlike movies where one might expect to see a movie once and then not see it again for several months or years, our games are expected to provide a new experience every time our consumers decide to sit down and begin a game once again. This value is increased if they enjoy the experience so much that they look forward to playing a new game several times a week or even a day. Additionally, there is an expectation that through our games you can meet other folks like yourself who have similar interests as you. And finally, since we are in the business of creating collectible games, the expectation is that each purchase is an investment. That investment only provides value if the consumer has confidence that the game brand will be available to participate in years from now or if the value of older out of print sets go up in value over time. In the collectible game business when you provide these value propositions you can create long-term consumers that are incredibly valuable to the brand.

In addition to being an entertainment product, oftentimes our products are actually based on forms of entertainment such as movies, books, or comics.

For example, we have a game called HeroClix. It is a collectible miniatures game where people purchase booster packs of randomized miniatures that they can then use to create their own game experience with their friends. For our fans, this is a wonderful sort of entertainment. It just so happens that this line is all based on licenses from Marvel, DC Comics, and Dark Horse Comics, which they also read as a form of entertainment. The popularity of these media properties can have a direct impact on the success or failure of our product line as well as take time-share away from our products. There are many other games within our category that have a direct causal link to some media property, and as the popularity of the media property goes, so can the product line. It becomes an important part of our job to create an entertainment experience that stands well on its own so that fans play our games for the game's sake and not just because they were initially attracted to the license that is attached to the game.

Finally, all our games are collectible. In order for them to be collectible, there needs to be enough "items" to collect, a reason to want to collect them, and enough of a challenge to collecting all of the items so that fans feel like they are part of an elite group when they successfully collect a set. The challenge for us is to create a new product where there are enough items to collect, but not too many, and to have the print run of the product be limited to a certain amount that is neither too little nor too much. Each product is different in this regard pending on who the target audience is for the product. For example, the cost to collect a product that we plan to create for eight- to twelve-year-olds will be much lower than that of a product intended for purchase by twenty-four to thirty-five-year-olds. We need to ensure that the difficulty to collect is not so high that consumers get discouraged, but not so easy to collect that they have no secondary market value. The balance for this is a fine line that we spend a tremendous amount of time and statistics in order to properly manage.

The WizKids Development Plan

Our development plan is fairly simple yet radically different from where we were previously: find out what the consumer wants, find out how the retailer needs to have it delivered so they can confidently sell it, and then execute. In the past we would often create products that we would personally like, assuming that since we are gamers if we liked it then by the transitive property of equality, so would other gamers. Given that we don't have a single game designer under the age of twenty-five, and our employees have more disposable income than the average twelve- to seventeen-year-old and are more sophisticated in terms of understanding strategy game options than the average twelve- to seventeen-year-old, what may be interesting to us from a personal standpoint could be radically different than what a twelve-year-old thinks. Embracing this concept has helped us move the company to become extremely consumer focused and to create new games that are achieving a much higher level of consumer satisfaction in the marketplace.

Leading this charge is the challenge. As with many companies in our category, the company had different heads at the top of each department for sales, marketing communications, game development, and brand management, which can create functional silos. With all of these groups reporting directly to one person, we have been able to give the leader of each group better guidelines for their responsibilities while at the same time giving each one the ability to share insights with each other, receive constructive criticism more easily, and work in a more collaborative fashion as each of these disciplines is actually a part of the same team. We have encouraged each of the directors to have regular lunches with each other. The theory is that when you can relate to your coworkers on a personal level it makes it easier to discuss issues and conflicts when they arise as you think of them as people and not as adversaries. Additionally, we have also experimented with our directors helping to mediate discussions between other directors in an effort to create an environment of group cooperation and discussion. These efforts are leading to a collaborative process where all of the groups realize they contribute to the equity of our brands and need to support this process.

How WizKids Approaches the Industry: A Different Philosophy

At WizKids, the primary focus is always on the consumer. There are other companies who make collectible games, however my impression is that they do things in the old Bell Labs way of research and development. That scenario consists of scientists sitting in a room coming up with "great new ideas." Once they have an idea established, they turn the idea over to the marketing department regardless of whether the idea can be achieved within a reasonable cost structure that could lead to a reasonable price. This does not take into account the perception of the consumer if this new idea is innovative or interesting. With the competition getting fiercer in collectible games and the shelf space getting more crowded, this seems like an extremely risky way to go about the business. At WizKids, this approach is simply not an option, and so we are constantly trying to improve our approach and look towards companies like Procter and Gamble and Unilever to truly understand how they manage their brand portfolios and launch new products.

Ensuring Profitability

While we believe at WizKids that our future growth will be through the development of more brands that we own, we understand there exists opportunities through smart licensing that can earn us short-term growth and profits while we execute against our long-term plan. With this in mind, we have one person dedicated to staying on top of trends, new properties coming up in the United States and Japan, and old properties that may be making a resurgence in the media. By staying on top of these trends it allows us to make smart bets on media properties that could provide us with explosive short-term growth.

Another part of ensuring that the company continues to generate profits is to pay close attention to the brands that we currently own. At Wizkids, we are in the process of building up our capabilities to create new IPs that can be leveraged into media properties down the road as well as have all of the necessary ingredients for creating a great game experience. One challenge that we have is that many successful media properties don't actually translate well into the game experience. Creating these properties ourselves ensures that we can have an exciting storyline as well as a property suitable for a great game concept.

Launching New Products

The value of the collectible game category is that our fans treat our releases like movie fans treat the release of a new film. If a movie is coming out and they want to see it, they go see it. They don't wait for Christmas to see it. In this way, our niche is not seasonal unlike many toy and game properties that launch only at Easter or Christmas (the two biggest sales spikes during the year). If we do our jobs properly and create an energized fan base, they will buy product the month we put it out and not wait for a specific season.

That being said, as with any consumer product, there are some months that are better than others. If we are launching a product for the Core Hobby Game market, it makes sense to coincide the launch with Gen Con, the largest Core Hobby Game consumer event of the year. If the property is somewhat broader, we may want to launch it at San Diego ComicCon, which has turned into the largest pop culture consumer event. Otherwise we are looking at space in the marketplace when our competitors are not doing big launches and when we currently do not have offerings planned.

Pricing Strategies for the Toys and Games Industry

In the collectible game industry, pricing strategy is simple:

1. For trading card games: Look at the price of Yu-Gi-Oh and Magic and price your product accordingly.
2. For role playing games: Look at the price of Dungeons and Dragons and price accordingly.
3. For miniatures games: Look at the price of HeroClix and Star Wars and price accordingly.

The reality of pricing strategy is that most companies in our niche of the game industry cannot afford in-depth pricing studies, so it is essential to look at the marketplace and match and compare prices rather than study or innovate. Even if you had the data that proves a new pricing approach, I'm not sure the majority of retail outlets would believe it or embrace it.

Deciding the Right Price for the Product

By looking at the channel of distribution, the age of the target consumer, the competitive set that we will fit into, and the range of SKU offerings that we will be presenting, we are best able to decide on the right price for a product. It is important that there be a product rationale for why you would purchase each SKU and we don't want to shift sales from one SKU to another because of price advantage. We are in the collectible business and we want the value proposition for collecting a particular piece to be the same across all SKUs.

Currently, our price range for products range from $3.49 a booster pack for a trading card game all the way up to $85 for a single colossal figure that plays in our miniatures game. We may change prices when we truly launch new products or categories or when there is movement on prices within the marketplace. At times, this can be less than once a year.

Since typically companies do not lower their prices in our niche of the industry—they've only gone up over time—the competitor's pricing has little impact on the price range for our products. If our competitor raises their prices we have two opportunities: raise ours with them or capitalize on the fact that we don't "need" to raise our prices. The first option increases profitability to us, the other increases good will from our retailers and consumers and can increase overall sales volumes and support. We employ the strategy that works best for us at the time. Other external variables that may have a significant impact on our pricing strategies are inflation, oil costs, and wage hikes at manufacturing vendors.

Many companies use incentive or marketing techniques to encourage a consumer to want to buy our product. There is a problem that plagues our industry though, and that is the Internet. While we all know that it is a great tool in terms of creating increased distribution opportunities and that it is here to stay, it does create problems for our business.

Our games work best in a brick and mortar environment. Our products can show their true value better in person than through jpegs on a Web site. People are more energized when they run into other enthusiasts at the store than when they shop alone. Fans who play the game more often buy more product and they have the opportunity to meet other fans and play games with them at brick and mortar stores than they do online. So the challenge for us is that what is best for growing and sustaining our brands is having people go into stores and meet other enthusiasts. When brick and mortar retailers perceive that they are losing sales to the Internet, they pull their support for these games, which is contrary to what is actually needed to support these games for the enthusiasts.

Last year we started a "Buy it By the Brick" program. If you bought a "brick" (twelve boosters) of one of our miniatures games from a "brick" and mortar store, you could send in your receipt and a coupon that would make you eligible to receive a free, exclusive figure that could only be obtained through this program. It not only increased initial purchases from our fans but also pushed them back to brick-and-mortar stores, which the retailers greatly appreciated.

The responsibility for determining pricing strategies at WizKids is somewhat of a joint task between sales, brand management, and me. Brand management focuses on the internal pressures that would make it necessary to raise prices while sales looks at what the competitors are charging retail. When a change pops up, these groups get together to discuss if a change is needed on our end, and if so, when is the most natural time to implement that change for both the retailer and the consumer.

In general, there are five key components that affect your pricing strategies:

1. Competitive landscape
2. Costs
3. Retailer acceptance
4. Target consumer
5. Type of game product

Competitive landscape: Who are your competitors? What are they charging for similar products? How strong are their brands? Your products have to logically fit within the preconceived pricing notions that these competitive products create in the minds of consumers.

Costs: Is this a lost leader for our company or a cash cow? Is this a one time opportunity based on a short-term license, or is this a long-term property that we will create a franchise around? The answers to these questions will determine the level of profit that we will accept for this particular game offering.

Retailer acceptance: Is the retailer familiar with this product or is it so innovative that they have nothing to base their own personal projections against? Is this a license that the retailer has many fans for or is it something unknown to them? Not all licenses are created equal and the retailer knows it. Star Wars garners more attention and confidence than the cartoon that plays at 2:00 a.m. on weeknights.

Target consumer: Are they old or young? What is their disposable income? What are all of the entertainment competitors for their free time? Some games have fans that will spend over $1,000 a year on new products. That fan is not eight years old. Pending the target you are going after will determine what price points can be supported.

Type of game product: Consumers have perceptions about various game formats. While it may be okay for a Trading Card Game to have a purchase model like where you buy numerous packs over and over, for board games the expectation is that you buy the first one this year, and the follow-up expansion or new version a year from now. When innovating a category you have to know what the expectations are of the target consumer before building your business and pricing model.

Adding Financial Value to the Company

Three things add value to WizKids from a financial standpoint:

1. Increase excitement for current products
2. Create new games that last beyond one release
3. Refine planning and execution to decrease wasted costs

It is an important business objective to excite and surprise fans with each new release. It is not enough to just exist and create a new set of "items." We must actually find ways to create new game concepts that change the way our players think about game strategy with each release. This is a challenge, but certainly not impossible, and the more ways in which we create new game concepts, the better the results. If we can do this with our current products we make greater gains than launching a new product as we already spent the time and effort up front of creating the existing business years ago and can now reap the downstream rewards.

In our part of the industry one truly reaps the rewards on collectible games when you can create a long-term business with multiple releases every year for several years. If you create a game that goes one release and then it's done, you don't get to amortize the start-up costs for these businesses and those costs can be quite costly. Unfortunately that has been a growing trend within our collectible games sector of the game industry and at WizKids we are working to reverse that trend.

Increasing Efficiencies

Every company needs to work on increasing efficiencies and removing waste from their process. We want to do this without removing what makes our games exciting to fans in the first place. Our mantra is "cost in, value out," meaning if you're going to put the cost in it should only be because the perceived value from the consumer is greater than that original cost. On the other side, if it provides no additional value to the consumer and does not increase sales, pull it out. We recently had a product that we pulled back and reviewed before production. By adding a map and some play scenarios, which were low cost both in physical terms and in internal resource terms but high in perceived value by the consumer, we literally doubled our sales orders, which increased our economies of scale and overall revenue. As we get better at understanding our value propositions to consumers and can plan for these up front, we will increase sales while decreasing activity costs to arrive at the right product configurations.

Factoring Efficiencies into the Leadership Plan

All of this aids in creating focus within the organization. Prior focus was on launching multiple new products each year in order to create all of the additional revenue needed for growth. This is not the most efficient way to go about fixing problems though, as it only works if all of the new products succeed or if one of them becomes a huge hit. If neither of these scenarios occurs then the company is actually worse off then previous as you probably removed your focus from what was working fairly well to create these new products that don't work at all. This is when you realize that the bird you had in the bush flew away. By moving towards this approach we are working towards creating a larger revenue base from brands that we currently know work and that will allow us to make targeted attacks on the category with new products that will have a higher chance of success.

Taking Market Share Away from Other Companies

Like all brands, games have hard core enthusiasts at the center and consumers at the fringe who may be participating not because they are 100 percent satisfied with the brand but because it's the closest to what they want and their friends participate in the brand. Imagine the hard core enthusiasts of Harley Davidson. Do you think you can easily persuade someone who is a huge Harley fan to switch to a cute and sporty Honda? Probably not. I'm not sure you could do it with a big burly Honda either. So much of Harley's appeal is in the personality traits that the brand transfers on to the owner. This is the same for many games in our category. The hard core enthusiasts would not think of changing games because the game helps define who they are as an individual. But there are people out on the fringe who can be moved over if you study what their dissatisfaction is with their current brand and then create and communicate product offerings that overcome these shortfalls provided by the competition.

Incorporating Market and Client Feedback into the Process

At WizKids, we typically share all market and client feedback information within the entire company. We recently made a radical change to one of our products by adding super rare figures into the set. These figures were based on a comic series by Marvel that was hugely popular and kept secret from the fans until someone opened up a booster pack and received one of the figures. The industry went nuts. Our brand manager for HeroClix would personally give informational updates to the entire organization regarding the progress of the promotion. This was important for two reasons. First of all it was a great morale boost to everyone in the organization as they had worked on the project. Secondly, it allowed us to consolidate the important information regarding the progress of the promotion and customer satisfaction and give it to everyone at the same time. This way everyone knew what they could and couldn't say publicly, as well as what our next steps would be to continue pushing the value of this promotion forward.

For other types of feedback, we are in the process of instituting roundtable discussions with all of the consumer teams to walk through the comments and come to an agreement about the true meaning behind what is being said by our constituents and what does this mean in terms of future strategy and execution.

Building an Effective Team

There are many aspects that go into building the ideal team for a company like ours. The ability to think strategically is probably the most important of these aspects. It is a tough skill to teach someone and it is one of the most important. Too much time and money gets wasted each year on tactics that don't actually solve a strategic problem or contribute to increasing brand equity or performance. As such, it becomes incredibly important in identifying this trait in potential new hires. Typically, we ask the various candidates a series of problem-solving questions during the interview process. If they are able to break down the problem into its various components and discuss a number of solutions along with the potential cause and effects to the solutions then we know that we have someone that has the basic foundation for strategic thought.

Another important aspect is the ability to learn. Many employees believe they know everything already. Realistically, no one knows everything. I personally strive to keep an open mind that today someone could teach me something new. It could be my boss, our administrative assistant, or the UPS guy delivering packages. If one is open to the idea that they could be exposed to something new that can help them in the future you would be amazed at how much you can learn in a day.

Being a team player who is capable of receiving constructive criticism and leaving the ego at the door, is the next important skill I look for in a team member. This is tied with the ability to learn. If you can not take constructive criticism, then it makes it very difficult for you to hear where others perceive your weaknesses, which makes it very difficult for you to improve both in a real sense as well as in the eyes of your peers and superiors. Without these three, you may have a person who is unwilling to learn and grow or do what is right for the company over what they want for themselves.

Measuring Success

At the end of the day, revenue growth and profit growth are the only metrics that matter when measuring success. That is the game that we play everyday with our business, especially if you work for a publicly-held company. However, in order to achieve both of those successes, it means you have to create products that consumers want and that retailers want to support. So we monitor fan and retailer forums to find out what they like and don't like about our ongoing efforts. We try to communicate what we are doing to fix the problems and then we fix them. We monitor industry magazines to measure how collectible our products are in relationship to the competitors' products. We monitor how our retail penetration is versus the competition, and so on. All of these factors, if monitored and pushed, lead to increased revenues, and if we are managing our company properly, increases profitability.

Strategies for Success

As a group we have focused on the following guidelines, which can be looked at as strategies:

1. Grow and refine our current brands
2. Value cost
3. Focus on the consumer

In the collectible game business, the greatest rewards are reaped from brands that have longevity and staying power. In the past, WizKids has been great at launching games but not as good at maintaining game brands. Our new focus is to shape our internal talents and processes in order to become better at this discipline so that we can fully amortize the start-up costs for creating new games and realize their full revenue potential.

Value cost is an ongoing challenge for any business and is the fundamental basis for the success of Wal-Mart. If a component does not provide value to the consumer, why should or would they want to pay for it? However, sometimes you can add a component that has far more value than its cost. By making the company acutely aware of these differences, our goal is to cut down on activities and costs that are ineffective and look for creative new ways to provide value to our consumers.

Both of these previous goals can only be achieved by focusing on the consumer. If we truly accept the fact that we need to communicate with the consumer in order to best serve them, then we will be able to find creative value adds for our products and create brands that can stand the test of time.

Qualities for Long-Term Success

It is important for a successful chief executive officer (CEO) to possess what Jim Collins calls a "Level Five Leader" in his book *Good to Great.*

In his book, Collins lists a good leader as one who is humble, one who takes criticism well, one who does what is right for the organization even if it means self-sacrifice, and one who doesn't necessarily have all of the answers but surrounds him or herself with people who have pieces of the answer.

If you are in the toy and game business for the long haul, at some point you will have to make some very tough decisions that may be personally unpleasant. You have to be able to do what is best for the organization and take some lumps in order to ensure that your company will endure the rough times and changes in the marketplace. Being a Level Five Leader will help prepare one for these inevitable rough times.

Another quality is being open to learning. I had the good fortune of working with Dr. Richard Garfield, the inventor of the Trading Card Game category with his game "Magic: The Gathering." He once told me he always tries to adopt the role of the student no matter what situation he is in. Through not always believing that he knows everything, he raises his opportunity to learn something new. I strive to do this on a regular basis and it allows me to truly enable my staff to present new ideas and fully evaluate them rather than dismiss them because they may be similar to something I have experienced in the past that didn't work. Maybe the previous execution was flawed in some way or wasn't right for that consumer and maybe this new solution addresses those previous issues.

Advice to Pass on to Others

One important piece of advice I find myself passing on to other members of my teams is to understand what motivates people. Oftentimes we come up with the "right" answer based on rational and logical thought. Even the most rational and logical people have hot buttons of things that bother them. When presented a logical solution that hits a hot button even these most rational people can allow themselves to make poor decisions. I believe it is the responsibility of the presenter to bring these people around to the presenter's point of view. By understanding what motivates or distresses people ahead of time, most of the potential conflict that could have been created can actually be avoided. This makes for a much more cooperative and pleasant work environment.

The Best Piece of Advice Received

Probably the best piece of advice I have received with regard to my position is to not put up with shoddy management. This is good in two aspects. If you are a subordinate, don't use poor management as an excuse for you to not perform at a high level. Find creative and constructive ways to get things done. I wouldn't be here today if I had not taken that advice to heart. On the flip side, it's great advice as a manager. It is a constant reminder to me that I should not be a poor manager and it inspires me to do the right thing no matter how personally painful it may be for me at that time.

Facing Challenges

In business, we are always working with imperfect information. The challenge is making timely decisions in order to hit important releases knowing full well that at some point you will receive more information that will highlight the issue more clearly. When that happens, and it turns out that your earlier decision was optimal, that's great. But when you find out you can make a refinement to increase your odds of success that is when the internal turmoil starts. It really comes down to what is the expected increase of sales due to making the change versus what is the cost in time, money, and morale to make the change.

Again, even this information is not perfect. Typically we get all the leaders of the affected groups in a room and we discuss. If we have all of the pertinent information at the meeting, we make a decision at the end of the meeting. We all know that it is a decision making the best of a less than ideal situation but we all hang together on the decision. If we don't have all of the pertinent information, we identify what information we could actually get, set a quick deadline, and then make the final decision. The important thing is to stay swift on the decision. Sometimes we fall into paralysis by analysis, but we make best efforts to avoid this.

Misconceptions Surrounding the Industry

There is one misconception in this industry that CEOs of toys and games companies sit around all day brainstorming crazy ideas and directly create new toys and games. This may be true at very small, privately-held companies, but it is my experience that as the company grows or goes public it is not advantageous for the company as a whole for that activity to continue at the CEO level. While executives may have some occasional input into the creative process, we are largely spending our time analyzing the business, mentoring our middle managers, and answering interview questions.

These impressions exist because that is what Hollywood portrays the position to be, and in addition, wishful thinking on the part of folks who wish they were the CEO of a toy or game company.

Keeping the Competitive Edge

To keep a competitive edge in this business, it is important to take every opportunity to stay on top of the industry. Every morning there are three industry Web sites I visit to get the news blurbs of the day. I have employees who scan the fan and retailer industry forums and alert me to potential issues, which I then visit myself. Keeping up on reading industry magazines every month to foster a working knowledge of what is out there is also an important aspect of keeping a competitive edge. Frequent calls to distributors, retailers, and other executives in the industry help keep my ear to the ground on other developments. Finally, I play games with my friends and relatives so I can see how they interact with products. For some people it may be embarrassing to sit for an hour with a friend's six-year-old son talking to him about Pokemon cards, but for me it provides a wealth of qualitative insights as to the perceptions of my future consumers.

Golden Rules

There are three golden rules I strive to follow:

1. Be a Level Five Leader.
2. Adopt the role of the student.
3. Allow your creative experts to be creative.

The first two items tie back to what I believe is the ideal employee and a CEO should be the ultimate ideal employee. The concept of the Level Five Leader is one who checks their ego at the door and is willing to do what is necessary for the benefit of the organization despite the fact that the outcome may be personally uncomfortable for you. If you adopt the role of a student, you will always ensure that you will learn and grow and each day you will become better able to lead the organization into the future. And finally, while it is important to have a creative thinking CEO, there are many other responsibilities that a leader has to perform. Sometimes it is tempting for a leader to jump in and "help" with the creative process for new product ideas. Occasionally this leads to new ideas. Oftentimes this leads your actual creative staff to retreat, hide their ideas in fear of having their ideas easily dismissed, or become yes men to the CEO as they become afraid to give their boss negative feedback and constructive criticism too often. Set the long-term strategies for your company and let your creative staff find innovative ways to create new products that satisfy these strategies. Having a team of creative employees working together on new ideas will always yield better results than relying on one "mastermind" to solve everything.

In addition, look at what other successful companies do both in the toy and game industry and outside of the industry. Try to dissect what actually works well from both and then merge that together in a fashion that works for your own particular niche of the toy and game industry. Don't reinvent the wheel, just make better tires.

Joe Hauck is an eleven-year veteran of the core hobby game industry. He spent over ten years of his career at Wizards of the Coast, a wholly owned subsidiary of Hasbro where he rose through the ranks to become the vice president of brand marketing in charge of Magic: The Gathering, their flagship brand with retail revenues of over $300 million worldwide. In this role he oversaw the two best revenue years in Magic's history, led the business development of Duel Masters, the number-one trading card game in Japan from 2001 to 2005, and led the business development of Magic Online, the first financially successful online game to sell unique digital assets as its exclusive revenue model. Mr. Hauck moved to WizKids Games, a wholly owned subsidiary of Topps, in May 2006 to become the executive vice president of sales, marketing, and product development. WizKids is the creator of the collectible miniatures game category in which HeroClix is their flagship brand. WizKids also created the constructible strategy game category with the introduction of the game Pirates of the Spanish Main. Along with new president Lax Chandra and new executive vice president of finance and operations Jeff Clark, they are transforming WizKids to become a disciplined market driven company that focuses on collectible games.

Challenges in the Toy and Game Industry

Arete Passas

President and Chief Executive Officer

Manhattan Toy Company

Presidential Challenges

People probably think being the president of a toy business is all fun and games, but this is first and foremost a business. Yes, it is great to be in a business that makes people smile, but the challenges of this business are as tough as any other kind of business. To those people who perhaps think it is just easy and fun, yes, it is fun, but no, it is not always easy.

I have worked in other consumer businesses. The toy business is the consumer business, it just happens to be toys. There is an unpredictable nature to the business. A movie, cartoon, book license or a new product can drive up the energy around that product or brand in ways that we do not plan or could not predict. When *Groovy Girls* dolls were first introduced in 1998, they were just some soft dolls in the Manhattan Toy line of product and we didn't know at the time that they would become an enduring and popular brand for girls. There are surprises in this business that do not often happen in other categories, and you cannot necessarily plan for those surprises. There are good and bad surprises, so you need breadth in your product portfolio to let you manage the spikes and the dips, which are going to be more severe than they are in other businesses. You need to work at developing an ability to predict which products will be a hit. You also always need to keep in mind the seasonality of the business, which tends to be in the fourth quarter of the year, as opposed to other businesses like toothpaste or tuna fish that don't necessarily have seasonal spikes.

This job is challenging simply because so much is always going on within the company, so many details to oversee and consider. We have over 500 items out on the shelves at any one time, so that adds up to many details to handle, trying to be sure we cross all the t's and dot all the i's as best we can. You have to be fast and you have to be smart in this business, but sometimes things get through, and it is frustrating when we know we could have done better on something. It is a challenge to juggle everything we are doing, get it all done on time, and do a great job.

Another challenge is determining the opportunities for growth. How can you predict the next area for growth? Toys and games are not the kind of thing where you can go to consumers and ask what kind of toys they would like. With other categories of merchandise, you can find out, not necessarily what they would like, but the attributes of some products they like or need in that category. That is not necessarily the way it is in toys, because toys are about engaging children, making them happier or smarter or more creative, and making them smile. These benefits are less tangible and predictable and are comprised of an emotional connection between the consumer and the toy.

What makes our company different from others in the toy business? We are positioned as a global marketer of toys that feature innovative designs to inspire imaginative play in today's kids. That is our mission statement. The difference is we are not a company that wants to be all toys to all kids, or even all toys to a certain group of kids. We focus on highly innovative designs for imaginative play, so it also means that we intend to be a higher price point than our competitors.

The roots of our business are in independent specialty toys. We have evolved into the mass market channels with Target and Toys R Us, but the foundation and strength of our business is still in the independent specialty toy channel. This also sets us apart from our competition. Many much larger companies are everywhere you can find a toy, and that is their strategy. We are not one of the big players, and we like that, because it gives us a sharper, more unique positioning in the marketplace.

The growth plan for our company begins with building on the foundation of the strong brands that we have, which include the *Groovy Girls* brand and our baby brands, like *Whoozit*. The second part of the plan is introducing new products into target markets we already reach, such as moms of babies and young girls who are attracted to the Groovy Girls line. This is done through internal development as well as through acquisition. A third area for growth is to continue to focus on awareness with the consumer through distribution, merchandising, promotion, and advertising.

As president, I focus on achieving and maintaining a clear, understandable vision for our company, and helping our people internalize it every day. I let people know where we are going and keep the focus on that. It is critical to be sure you have the right people in the right place to get you to your goals and to ensure that the company's resources are allocated toward achieving those goals.

To be sure we stay on track toward those goals, we monitor where we are on a regular basis. We look at the economic value of the company (EVA). We measure this EVA regularly, and that is measured by the ratio of our earnings before interest and taxes over capital employed in the business. We measure that monthly, to see how we are tracking and how that relates to the economic value added formula that we have. Ultimately, that is the acid test. We want to be sure we have a positive EVA for the company, and everything we do and the way we do it all relates to the ultimate question: are we increasing the value of the company?

Company Growth and Success

The clearest benchmark of success is revenue growth. We do not have a lot of sophisticated information relative to market share. If we did, we would be tracking share data, but we are too small to have that right now. We do read brand awareness levels. We go online yearly and track our awareness level, both aided and unaided, because we know our success is going to be linked with the level at which moms and girls are aware of our products.

We daily monitor our sales level, in terms of bookings, what our retail customers have ordered versus what we have shipped to customers, which are actual sales. We monitor that against all our customer types, whether a specialty independent customer or a national account like Target. We track that versus the prior year, and we can see if we are up or down. We look at it by product category and individual items within a product category, so we would break out our *Groovy Girls* business from our general Plush business, from our baby business. Also, we look at the trends over the past three or four years in the business, both in terms of year-to-year and month-to-month, so we keep a very close eye on the retail piece of things. Along with that, we monitor the associated expenses relative to those retail sales versus the prior year, to see that we are on track in terms of what we are spending and what we are getting for our spending.

Growth also means taking market share from our competitors or growing a category. This is possible through the strength of the product or the brand that we bring to market. So in the case of the Groovy Girls brand, we are able to expand the market of dolls into "soft dolls." A new category like this can expand the market as it gives little girls and their moms an alternative to the leading dolls out there. The *Groovy Girls* dolls are funky yet fashionable and allow a girl to express herself. They foster individuality and friendship and they have a wholesome appeal. These attributes appeal to moms as well as to the girls.

As stated earlier, new products are an important part of our company plan. New products are the life blood for the toy industry. Unlike some consumer products companies that would spend a lot of time and money in research and development, our company decides on new products more in terms of good ideas. We look at new ideas with our professional and parental eye. If we think something makes sense, if it is consistent in growing our strategy—is this in our sweet spot, are we already talking to this target group—then we bring out a product. We might or might not have focus groups with moms and/or children discussing the item. We might or might not have shown it in some daycare centers to see if children get engaged with playing with the item. We are a smaller company so this can be an advantage in the quick way we can make decisions as a management team. We can and should be nimble and faster to market than our larger competition.

In the development of new products, there is no formulaic approach in terms of regularly researching things. However, with major new items, introductions, or perhaps a category or a type of product that we are going to introduce for the first time, we would research with moms and/or with kids first. New products definitely drive the business, because it is all about what is new. We add new products to current lines to freshen the line. Our *Groovy Girls* dolls change every six to twelve months, to bring new dolls to the shelf. In many ways, it is like the fashion or cosmetic business since there is a constant freshening of ongoing lines as well as the introduction of new lines or items.

Earlier, I mentioned the challenge of predicting the next phase of growth, determining what customers want in our product. Client feedback is very important. We do talk to our target market and we do test new products in daycare centers or by talking to mothers and/or children. Retailer feedback is very important to us. With many of our larger customers and many independent specialty retailers, we talk with them on a regular basis as well as in special meetings. We bring them together as a group and show them the kinds of products we are looking at for the future and get their response and their suggestions on product, positioning, packaging, and pricing. We recently modified the "eyes" on one of our doll lines due to consumer and retailer feedback that was consistent in suggesting a change.

With our larger customers, we consider them partners. We might talk with them today about something that will happen a year from now. We constantly stay in touch with what they look for in terms of margins, new items in the category, and what they see from shoppers in their stores. This is a very close partnership with our sales group and our key retailers in the marketplace, this constant talking back and forth, and they see things well before we even decide if we are going to produce them.

Basics of Pricing

At our company, the heads of marketing, business development, operations, and I work together to monitor pricing. Sales and finance are in there as well, but normally the responsibility rests with the business development and marketing team. The prices of our key products range as low as $5 retail, all the way up to $100 retail, but the average of most of the items would probably be between $20 and $25, but that depends on which line you are looking at. Our Groovy Girls line is lower than that.

In the toy industry, pricing is balancing the margin that we are trying to get out of the product and with where the product is going to be in the marketplace and how will it be seen versus similar, competitive items. Our positioning is a better/best positioning, and we will always be at the higher end of the spectrum in terms of price comparisons, but so often with items we compete against and the categories we compete in, price is not necessarily a key factor.

If you are picking up a plush toy, for example, you are not necessarily looking at it to make sure you are getting a $14.99 plush toy, but rather you look at it and look into the eyes of the character and see if you want it or not. Price is more of a factor in categories where there is more competition, particularly bigger companies that offer a broad line. Since most of our competition is significantly larger than we are, we can get a fair bit of pricing pressure. This forces us to stay in areas where we know we can compete well, as opposed to trying to go head-on in some of the more competitive areas.

Sometimes we will get feedback from consumers in early research about what pricing they would expect to pay for something. Ultimately it does relate to a margin we need to have and you look at your margins on a total product portfolio basis. You may be able to have a sharper margin on one line because you are carrying a greater margin elsewhere. If it is a quality product, and mom and the child want it, pricing will not necessarily be a big deterrent as it can be in other categories, particularly where there is price comparison shopping. No one else has our identical product. Yes, there are other dolls and stuffed animals, but not the same specific ones as ours, so there is a little more flexibility in many parts of the toy business in regard to pricing.

The expected return on investment does have some impact on the pricing as well. We look at earnings before interest and taxes over capital employed. That is our measure and that relates to a positive EVA. Basically, if you are going to invest in some tooling for a plastic item of some kind, you want to get some return at least within eighteen months. Pricing is as important at the top end as the low end. You don't want to price something too low such that the consumer does not see it as a quality item. Too low a price can cheapen a product. It is not necessarily about the price of an item in the consumer's eye but rather about the value she is getting.

An external variable that impacts our pricing strategies is our suppliers. They have minimum order quantities for which we can manufacturer a product, so we have to do certain levels of production. If they are going to manufacture something for us, it has to be a certain order size or it is not going to be affordable. Our suppliers are constantly getting cost pressures on the cost of labor or materials so we always have to factor that in and build it in as we are designing the product. High volume can certainly change your pricing structure. We have had products that were initially only sold in specialty at smaller quantities at higher prices. When we redesigned them for a larger customer and increased the volume tenfold, it changed the formula for our pricing such that we could bring the price down significantly and still offer a high-quality product.

Price Changes and Promotions

When we do increase prices, usually this is a result of a significant product improvement. We seldom increase pricing on a permanent item in the line. Normally, once we come out with an item, it stays for a couple of years. We do not necessarily have ongoing items that need price increases. New products are constantly being introduced—anywhere from 50 to 80 percent of the line turns over every year with new items so new items are constantly being introduced with new pricing.

It is unusual for us to have discounted products, because we like to have all our products across channels be the same price at every channel. Somebody cannot go into Target and buy an item cheaper than they can in an independent retail store. We have a minimum advertised pricing policy in which we say if you are going to advertise the product, you will advertise it at a minimum price. Sometimes the price does change for special offers or if there happens to be a promotion on an item and the retail customer can pass along a promotional discount, but that is a special circumstance.

We are not heavily promoted to the consumer. We rely on good retail placement, so we want to be very prominent in the store. We might do specific versions of the toy like a plush item. We might do a giant size of it that the retailer could feature to attract people into the store, and a smaller version of it inside the store. We will have merchandising vehicles. For instance, we supply special displays for our retailers to display the product well, whether it is a spinner rack that features puppets or something that will make it well merchandised so the consumer can easily shop the line.

Additionally, we do have advertising in consumer books for our baby product, to make consumers aware that we have the products, so they will shop for them. Our retail customers will run ads in newspapers, or their own circulars inform people about the product and encourage them to come into the store for a special item. Many times we will provide a gift with purchase so, for example, when you buy a *Groovy Girls* doll you get an accessory for free. And sometimes we will give extra product so the retailer can provide it to their customers as an incentive or gift with purchase.

There are many factors that determine the pricing of a product—cost, margin requirements, awareness, marketing/placement, promotions, competition—and they must be considered before making that decision. Creating a product that consumers want is only part of the strategy for success. Giving it to them at a price they are willing to pay is another.

The Management Team

The executives in our company who work with me toward attaining our goals fall into six major areas—all of equal importance.

The first is the head of business development and marketing. This is where all the ideas originate. We decide which products to make, how they will be priced, who they will be positioned for, which category, and so on. This is the area that oversees the design of all our products.

Next is the head of sales, both U.S. sales and international distributors. This group is responsible for growing our sales through new customers and existing customers and managing both internal and external sales reps.

Third, my managing director in the United Kingdom oversees our European business. Nearly 20 percent of our revenue comes from countries in Europe.

Fourth would be the operations area, which relates to getting our product produced, warehousing of our products, and all operating logistics. All our products are produced overseas, and operations work to see that we always get the best quality products at the best price and manage all the technical and quality details related to getting our products manufactured at our many suppliers.

The next area is finance and everything related to our financials including such things as our banking relationships, accounting, and credit to tracking our product P&Ls and developing business models for us to accurately evaluate our new initiatives.

The final area is the human resources area. It is all about the people we have in the organization, and I work closely with human resources to ensure that we have the right people and the right structure and the right compensation to keep a highly motivated work force.

When we add members to our team, the first thing I look for is passion. Do they have passion for what they do or what they are going to do? That is critical. In this business, you really have to have the emotional connection and passion for what you are doing. Secondly, I want experienced people. The toy business is different enough that experience is very helpful.

Third, I want people who possess the ability to work with people and to motivate a team. Can you lead a team and motivate them to be the best they can be? That is very important. When I interview someone, I ask myself if I would want to work for this person. If the answer is yes, then I usually think it is a good hire.

I often offer several pieces of advice to our team members. Keep innovating. Do not assume. When you are working with someone, do not assume they know what you are talking about or that they were going to take care of something. It may require some follow-up and a need to "check in." Another piece of advice is to listen. And lastly, never be afraid to admit or acknowledge that you do not know something, and if you do not know something, find someone who does. These are attributes I have found that can turn good managers into great managers.

The Future of the Toy Business

Most leaders in the toy business have been humbled over the past dozen years. At times, companies and/or individuals in those companies have been able to ride the wave, but there have been rude awakenings on a lot of fronts relative to either a brand or category suffering significant decline. One of the greatest challenges for the business overall has been the strength or growth of the electronics business with young children. Many children would rather sit and play with an electronic toy or on the computer versus playing with a teddy bear. This interest in electronics has crept into the younger age group where cell phones are being used well before the teen years. This leaves a tighter window in which children are interested in non-video toys and non-electronic toys. That has been a challenge for the toy business overall, and an ongoing challenge in the past few years. How individual companies face that challenge will affect their future. As for our company, my role will continue to set an achievable and understandable vision for the company and ensure we have the resources to get there.

I have been on board with this company for over a year now. I came from the outside, and changing the orientation of the business to focus on the consumer has been an ongoing, evolving process. This has been a challenge because people have always started the process by considering what the retailer wants or what a designer thinks might be cute or fun versus first thinking about the consumer and then backing into the retailers' needs. I think changing the mind-set of how people have looked at the businesses we are in and the businesses we should go into has been a challenge.

Part of this focus of determining what people want and giving it to them means staying on top of the industry. I read all the trade magazines and newspapers that come out, and the business journals, whether the *Wall Street Journal* or a business magazine. I go shopping a lot and observe everything from the grocery store to malls to department stores, just to stay in touch with what people are actually buying. You can learn a lot through observation. And this does not mean hanging out only in the toy department, but rather in the girls' clothing department and other areas to see where general consumer trends are going. I also read the consumer behavior books that come out and stay in touch with the magazines where we advertise.

A piece of advice I once received is important to how I carry out my duties. Keep learning and do not ever think you have learned it all. If you have, it is time to pack it in and retire. The day you feel you have learned everything is the day you stop growing and stop adding value to the business. So every single day I come to work, I think, "What will I learn today?" So keep learning. It is invigorating and it makes you better at everything you do.

To someone considering coming into this line of business, creating their own company vision or leadership plan, I offer this advice:

Be sure the vision is clear, crisp, and understandable, and then be sure you have people who can buy into the vision. Those two things are critical. Be sure the vision is realistic versus where you have been. Vision is always relative to where you are and where you are going. It is not like taking a company overnight from point A to point D, but rather from point A to point B. As time goes on, you need to constantly refine the vision and the expectations based on competitive conditions and things that have transpired in the marketplace—some you have initiated, and others you need to respond to.

Three golden rules for those who stand where I stand now: First, stay close to the consumer. Second, be prepared. Try to plan or protect yourself from surprises because in this business you can get a lot of them. And third, if you are not having fun, get out of it. This is the toy business, after all. If it doesn't make you smile and you can't get excited about funky dolls, fun to hold animals, or whimsical infant toys, then this is not the business for you.

A mother, former elementary school teacher, and Cornell University M.B.A. graduate, Arete Passas is president and chief executive officer of Manhattan Toy. Ms. Passas joined the Minneapolis-based manufacturer of the popular Groovy Girls dolls, Whoozit toys, and other innovative and creative playthings in June 2005. The twenty-five-year veteran of the children's and consumer products industries is guiding privately held Manhattan Toy's continued growth in the intense $35 billion worldwide toy market.

Over the years, Ms. Passas has developed and led strategic marketing campaigns for countless well-known consumer brands such as Oil of Olay, Scholastic, Dixie, Barbie, and Crayola. In fact, she is responsible for the first change in Crayola crayon colors in the brand's eighty-seven-year history and she introduced the popular "crayon tip" character that has become an enduring Crayola brand mark.

Most recently, Ms. Passas was vice president at ValueVision Media's ShopNBC.com division, in Eden Prairie, Minnesota where she was responsible for growth and management of the dot-com channel and served as a company officer. She oversaw numerous marketing initiatives, affiliate programs, design, content, and customer service.

Ms. Passas began her professional career in 1979 as marketing manager for Olay, Clearasil, Vidal Sassoon, Pantene, and Fixodent brands at Richardson Vicks, a subsidiary of Procter & Gamble, in Wilton, Connecticut. She managed the launch of the Olay Beauty Bar, and prepared market analysis, product concepts, and market entry strategy for the Olay cosmetic line that ultimately inspired P&G's acquisition of Noxell. In 1987, Ms. Passas joined Binney & Smith, a subsidiary of Hallmark's Crayola products division, where she managed new product marketing and revitalized the flagship crayon business. She concepted and managed the introduction of the COLOR WORKS line of crayon sticks, mechanical pencils and pens, and the introduction of Crayola's first coloring book line.

Ms. Passas was tapped to lead a start-up early childhood division at Scholastic Inc. in New York in 1991. She developed and launched the company's first preschool magazine and launched the division's first direct mail catalog. In the early nineties, Ms. Passas became director of marketing at James River Corporation in Norwalk, Connecticut, managing a $300 million tabletop business comprised of Dixie, Vanity Fair, Northern, and Zee brands. She led a 15 percent turnaround in the declining paper cup and plate categories and implemented three major new lines including holiday and children's items.

In 1994, Ms. Passas became vice president for Mattel's games and puzzles division in Syosset, New York, where she managed all domestic brand functions and international marketing for Uno, Barbie, and Disney. While at Mattel, Ms. Passas spearheaded new product introductions and line extensions and won Disney licensing rights for puzzles, a category first.

A native of Dover, New Hampshire, Ms. Passas has worked in the Twin Cities market since 1998 when she became executive vice president for Department 56, a popular fine collectibles and gifts company based in Eden Prairie, Minnesota. Ms. Passas led a variety of initiatives, including implementation and redesign of a stronger brand identity, the launch of the first branded advertising campaign, licensing agreements, and redesign of the company Web site. As general manager with Plymouth, Minnesota-based Halo Innovations, Ms. Passas created the new category vision and led the company's Infant Sleep Care line from start-up to a multimillion-dollar profitable entity in just three years. She obtained distribution for the relatively new brand in key mass outlets and helped raise dollars to fund working capital.

Ms. Passas holds an M.B.A. from Cornell University and a B.A., magna cum laude, from the University of New Hampshire. She currently serves on the board of the Girl Scout Council of Greater Minneapolis and is an active member of the Women Presidents' Organization.

Success in the Toy and Game Industry

Debra Fine

Chief Executive Officer

Small World Toys

The toy industry offers unique challenges in terms of effective management. We operate in the realm of consumer products; our job is to come up with quality brands and conduct focus group testing to make sure our brands are reaching our core audience. Most of the manufacturing end of our business is done in China; from there, we have to focus on selling our product to retail stores and supporting the retail process by packaging and marking the product correctly and spelling out features and benefits of product through in-store merchandising, promotions, and consumer marketing. What makes the toy industry unique in the consumer products marketplace is the simple fact that we are providing products for children; consequently, there is a whole other layer involved in the development and marketing processes. We must make sure our products are developed with youngsters' play patterns in mind. At the same time, we are marketing to parents as well as to children, so it is important that our toys achieve some kind of educational goal such as improving cognitive skills, small and large motor skills, and small and large motor skills cause and effect imaginative play. Toys and play are the most effective way to create critical connections and learning for children.

Achieving Corporate Goals

When I first bought this company, it was very well known as a distributor of high-end educational products for children; in the last two years we have gone on to develop our own lines of proprietary toy brands that teach children effectively. My goal was to create a company that produces well-known and well-respected product brands that create a fun-filled learning experience for infants, preschoolers, and youngsters up to the age of ten.

Many factors make our company unique: the educational value and high quality of our products; the special relationships that we have with our retailers and customers; and the fact that we have licenses for developing products based on the stories of Dr. Seuss and Eric Carle. In other words, we take very high-end, beloved authors and license their product, as opposed to spinning off products from movies and television shows—and because of this, our product line is evergreen. While you might not see a big blip in sales occur very often, our goal is to achieve product longevity. Having a core evergreen line of products allows you the financial base to develop innovative products and take some chances.

Success in this business stems from having a winning team at your side. When hiring management personnel, I look for self-starters—people who are strong, enthusiastic and detail oriented, but who can also see the bigger picture.

Checks and Balances

In order to ensure that corporate goals are being met, I meet with each of my department heads once per week. We discuss what our goals are—for example, how many millions in revenue and profits each brand should be able to achieve. This is based on historicals, new product, and an analysis of what we will sell into each channel such as specialty mass, chain, education, catalog, online and international accounts. We then conduct a slotting analysis—in other words, our marketing department pinpoints where there are holes in the market, what price points we need, and what features would add substance to a particular brand. A style guide is developed for each brand to make sure everything that goes into that line or brand of products further enforces the message of each product, whether it is designed for developmental or imaginative play. In essence, product development, sales and marketing work hand in hand.

Launching a Product

New product launches generally occur during certain key seasons for the toy industry. The annual Toy Fair is held in February, so the toy industry generally comes out with new products in January; these are products that sell well into the spring and summer. New toy introductions also take place in June; these toys are usually a bit more expensive, as they are aimed at fall and winter holiday sales.

However, the specialty industry—high-end stores and smaller mom-and-pop-type shops—operates on a different schedule than the big box retailers; these stores work nine to twelve months in advance to pick their product. Therefore, an event called the Mass Show is held in October so that those retailers can choose what products to order for Christmas of the following year.

Research and Development

What products will be the biggest hits at these annual trade shows? It all comes down to research and development. That process starts with market research—looking at what the demographic and psychographic audiences are for our products, and considering which consumers buy from which retailers. We definitely have a niche—our products are generally for households with $100,000+ income; both parents are usually working, college educated, and very cognizant of developmental play and products that educate but are also fun. We always keep the identity of our typical customer in mind.

Other factors we consider in the research and development process include price points and play patterns—for example, does this toy feature a unique or good play pattern for children to learn such as cause and affect or open-ended imaginative play? The competition's product line has to be factored in. We always look to acquire new licenses, but they have to be evergreen, such as licensing the work of a famous author. We also consult focus groups and subscribe to most of the marketing company research reports that do a very in-depth job of identifying consumers and their buying habits. Focus groups allow children to play fully with the product and show us what they like and don't like. We also conduct focus groups with parents to determine what features in products appeal to them the most.

In order to determine what our customers want or need we do a combination of things. We get our retailers and sales reps involved—they are out there in the retail channel all the time, so they know what does and does not sell. We help retailers do focus groups on what is and is not selling; we also conduct our own focus groups, talking to customers directly, and having children come in and play with new toys at our company. We use a focus group coordinator that brings in the target age group whether it be children or parents. She asks questions and shows product and we are behind a one-way mirror so we can watch reactions.

Increasing Market Share

The best way to increase market share is to do what you do best; if you develop good products for consumers and good marketing programs for retailers, you will increase your market share. Our strategy is not to look at what the competition is doing and try to copy their products and undercut their price. We are more focused on the quality of our brands and our relationships with our retailers, usually merchandising a full brand or line together on a shelf or display with shelf stalkers.

Thorough planning is a key to our success. We conduct a major operating plan meeting each year, and then review our plans halfway through the year. Around September we start planning all of our product introductions for January and what we think each product will do. We then check actual sales against projections on a monthly basis—did the product come out on time and on budget; and is it selling as much as we thought it would? We get margin reports on a regular basis, so that we can measure product performance in terms of sales and profitability. If the product is not performing we will take it out of our line. If the margin is low we will either work on lowering the cost of the product or raise the price.

The Role of the Toy Industry CEO

Meeting Challenges

One of the biggest challenges facing a toy company chief executive officer (CEO) in today's marketplace is the fact that most manufacturing is done in China. This long-distance manufacturing process can be fairly unpredictable; even if you are working with very good vendors, there are many things that could occur in the production process to make product runs late or more costly. It is very challenging to accurately predict how much inventory you will need and when you are going to need it, and to time production in such a way that you have inventory when you need it but you do not have too much. The whole inventory planning and production process is extremely challenging, and much more of a moving target than I would like it to be.

Increasing Shareholder Value

As CEO of a public company, you must always watch out for shareholder value; you have to make sure your decisions take into account what is going to be best for your shareholders in the short and long term. While in many cases the goals you want to set for your company involve long-term planning, as head of a public company you also have to consider what you need to do this quarter to make sure you give value to your shareholders. It is challenging to engage in long-term strategic planning for managing growth, when it might cost you shareholder value in the short term.

It can be especially challenging when you are in the type of situation I faced when I bought this company; it had been owned and operated by the same family for forty years. In order to achieve the type of growth that we have now, I had to persuade people who were used to doing things a certain way to grow, change, and try new methods.

Achieving Success

Certain qualities are necessary for achieving success as a toy company CEO. Among these are absolute persistence and the ability to formulate and communicate a sound, clear corporate strategy that is flexible enough to adapt to change. You need to take calculated risks and weigh whether the outcome will be favorable enough to make investing in a plan worthwhile. Being a successful CEO is all about using good judgment, making good plans and having a really good staff because you can never do it all on your own—your plan can be fantastic, but if half of your departments are unable to execute that plan properly, it is going to fail every time.

At the same time, it is important to advise your management team wisely. I always tell my staff to consider the implications of every decision; in other words, to look at the bigger picture—if you decide that in order to save money you are going to cut back on a product line, you need to consider the repercussions of that decision.

Keeping Your Edge: The Importance of Vision

The CEO's success also depends on keeping up with what is going on in the industry. I network quite a bit with those involved in the toy industry; I am an executive member of the Young Presidents Organization, whose members include many top CEOs in the toy industry. Being a marketing person I am always looking at current market research; I also glean a great deal of information from my board of directors.

Keeping your edge also involves maintaining your vision. Coming up with a vision for the company is an ongoing process that includes determining what the company's strengths are. You must then focus on those unique strengths and determine how you can capitalize on them to help your company achieve growth.

The Changing Role of the Toy Company CEO

Many years ago there were fewer barriers in terms of entry to the toy industry—if you had a product and if you had a good relationship with a group of retailers, you could sell the product; those retailers were not going to go to Europe or China to find products.

As time went by, big well-funded companies such as Mattel and Hasbro came in and acquired many other companies; competition in the industry became more sophisticated and fierce. These days, it is the bigger companies who, for the most part, are able to stay in business. Being more efficient and sophisticated has become more important, whereas when the industry was smaller, you could often be successful by just being creative and having nice looking products. At the same time, many of the smaller retailers have gone out of business; the ones who have survived are, like the toy industry itself, more sophisticated.

Increasingly, there are a lot of professional CEOs running the toy industry, as opposed to the people who actually founded the toy companies, because the industry has changed so much over the last few years.

Debra Fine, chief executive officer, combines an entrepreneurial spirit with a distinguished record of executive leadership. A three-time chief executive officer with over fifteen years of experience in consumer products, entertainment, and media, Ms Fine's background includes marketing, licensing, operations management, and creating growth in start-up ventures. Her expertise extends to strategic planning, brand building, product development, business development, and strategic alliances.

From 2000 to 2002, Ms Fine held the position of chief executive officer for Fandom Media, a "tween" products company until the company was acquired. Prior to that, she served as chief executive officer of Cloud 9 children's products. Additional leadership roles include vice president of marketing for Disney Interactive Products, vice president of strategy for Kraft, Quaker, and American Express for Marketing Corporation of America, and a director at EM Ventures, a venture capital fund.

Ms. Fine holds a B.A. in journalism and advertising from the University of Southern California and an M.B.A. from UCLA.

Management
Best Sellers

Visit Your Local Bookseller Today or Go to www.Aspatore.com
for More Information

- Corporate Ethics - Making Sure You Are in Compliance with
  Ethics Policies; How to Update/Develop an Ethics Plan for Your
  Team - $17.95
- Ten Technologies Every Executive Should Know - Executive
  Summaries of the Ten Most Important Technologies Shaping the
  Economy - $17.95
- The Board of the 21st Century - Board Members from Wal-Mart,
  Philip Morris, and More on Avoiding Liabilities and Achieving
  Success in the Boardroom - $27.95
- Inside the Minds: Leading CEOs - CEOs from Office Max, Duke
  Energy, and More on Management, Leadership, and Profiting in
  Any Economy - $27.95
- Deal Teams - Roles and Motivations of Management Team
  Members, Investment Bankers, Professional Services Firms,
  Lawyers, and More in Doing Deals (Partnerships, Mergers and
  Acquisitions, Equity Investments) - $27.95
- The Governance Game - What Every Board Member and
  Corporate Director Should Know About What Went Wrong in
  Corporate America and What New Responsibilities They Are
  Faced With - $24.95
- Smart Business Growth - Leading CEOs on Twelve Ways to
  Increase Revenues and Profits for Your Team/Company - $27.95

**Buy All 7 Titles Above and
Save 40% - Only $114.95**

Call 1-866-Aspatore or Visit www.Aspatore.com to Order

Other Best Sellers